Henry Martyn Hart

A Way that Seemed Right

An Examination of Christian Science

Henry Martyn Hart

A Way that Seemed Right
An Examination of Christian Science

ISBN/EAN: 9783744664264

Printed in Europe, USA, Canada, Australia, Japan

Cover: Foto ©Lupo / pixelio.de

More available books at **www.hansebooks.com**

"A Way That Seemeth Right."

Proverbs xvi., 25.

An Examination of "Christian Science."

BY

H. MARTYN HART, D.D.

Moderator and Medallist in Experimental and Natural Science, Trinity College, Dublin. Author of "A Manual of Chemistry," etc., and Dean of St. John's Cathedral, Denver, Colorado.

NEW YORK:
JAMES POTT & CO., PUBLISHERS,
FOURTH AVENUE AND TWENTY-SECOND STREET.
1897.

PREFACE.

In the work of my ministry I have found so many good people distressed by the specious seduction of this novel cult, "Christian Science;" so many families divided by it; so many dying persons sorely hindered by it; so many professing to have found peace through it; so many charlatans robbing the sick of their slender income by means of it, and so often have I been appealed to for advice and explanation concerning it; that I have, as a shepherd of the sheep, attempted to set forth in this book the unscientific nature of its pretensions, and at the same time to point out the natural explanation of its cures.

I pray God that, in His Mercy, He may be pleased so to bless this endeavor, that it may prove to those who are 'weak in the faith' a 'savour of life unto life' and an edification unto the Body of Christ.

H. MARTYN HART.

THE DEANERY,
DENVER, January, 1897.

CONTENTS.

CHAPTER I.
ON HEALING.

Miraculous Cures. Freedom from Sickness. The Power of the Devil. S. Paul's Infirmity of the Flesh. The Uses of Sickness. King Hezekiah's Rebellion against the Word of the Lord, and its Results. The Efficacy of Prayer.

CHAPTER II.
ON HEALING.

Lourdes. The Power of the Mind. Francis Schlatter and his Cures. A Peculiar Case.

CHAPTER III.
MIND AND MATTER.

Control of the Mind over the Body. Charming away Warts. Lord Bacon. The King's Evil. The Stigmata. Hypnotism. Instances of Hypnotism. A Miraculous Cure in Moscow. Influence of Personality. Cataract. Microbes. The Peculiar People. A Wonderful Cure Investigated. "Christian Science" Claims and Deeds.

CHAPTER IV.
"CHRISTIAN SCIENCE" HEALING.

The Subjective Mind. Instances of Its Working. Two Classes of Ailments. Microbic Diseases. Nervous Derangements. Absent Treatment. Effect of Sympathy. Communication between Minds. Mind Reading.

CHAPTER V.
THE DOCTRINE OF "CHRISTIAN SCIENCE."

The Sermon on the Mount. The Way of Salvation. Statement of "Christian Science."

CHAPTER VI.
MAN.

Mrs. Eddy's Meaning. Mortals and Mortal Minds the Creation of the Wicked One. Good and Evil. The Senses. Accurate Observation. Wickedness of Man. The Incarnation. The Divine Life.

CHAPTER VII.
THE HOLY GHOST.

The Ruler of this Dispensation. The Holy Ghost in the Bible : in Mrs. Eddy's book.

CHAPTER VIII.
SPIRIT.

Value of Terms. A Definition of Adam. Mrs. Eddy on Spirit. A False Syllogism. God is not all. Life and Spirit. Substance. The Substance of the Body. The Resurrection. Body of Our Lord. Ether. The Vortex Theory. Ether and Matter.

CHAPTER IX.
FORGIVENESS OF SIN.

The Gospel of Jesus Christ. Witnesses. The Christ Life. "Christian Science" and the Removal of Sin. The Divine Nature. The Teaching of "Christian Science" and the Gospel Contrasted.

CHAPTER X.
CONCLUSION.

The Value of "Christian Science." The Truth in "Christian Science." The Practice of "Christian Science" Healing. Hypnotism and Therapeutics.

CHAPTER V.
THE DOCTRINE OF "CHRISTIAN SCIENCE."

The Sermon on the Mount. The Way of Salvation. Statement of "Christian Science."

CHAPTER VI.
MAN.

Mrs. Eddy's Meaning. Mortals and Mortal Minds the Creation of the Wicked One. Good and Evil. The Senses. Accurate Observation. Wickedness of Man. The Incarnation. The Divine Life.

CHAPTER VII.
THE HOLY GHOST.

The Ruler of this Dispensation. The Holy Ghost in the Bible: in Mrs. Eddy's book.

CHAPTER VIII.
SPIRIT.

Value of Terms. A Definition of Adam. Mrs. Eddy on Spirit. A False Syllogism. God is not all. Life and Spirit. Substance. The Substance of the Body. The Resurrection. Body of Our Lord. Ether. The Vortex Theory. Ether and Matter.

CHAPTER IX.
FORGIVENESS OF SIN.

The Gospel of Jesus Christ. Witnesses. The Christ Life. "Christian Science" and the Removal of Sin. The Divine Nature. The Teaching of "Christian Science" and the Gospel Contrasted.

CHAPTER X.
CONCLUSION.

The Value of "Christian Science." The Truth in "Christian Science." The Practice of "Christian Science" Healing. Hypnotism and Therapeutics.

CHAPTER I.

ON HEALING.

IN February of this year, 1896, "The Christian Scientists" of New York opened a building which they had purchased for $75,000. This was the occasion of a long article by one of their number in "The New York Tribune" descriptive of the progress of the movement. The article said that already the sect had three hundred churches in the United States, and daily was increasing its number of adherents; that the particular congregation in New York was composed of eight hundred persons, all of whom had been cured of diseases more or less severe; and the writer would point us to the facts of these and similar cures as the corroboration of the theory upon which the "Science" is based. This theory in its present statement is due to a lady who says it was revealed to her in 1865, Mrs. Mary Baker G. Eddy. She stated the theory in her book, "Science and Health, with Key to the Scriptures," which was published in 1875, and has gone through more than one hundred editions.

It is not to be wondered at that so successful an authoress should have many imitators. To-day there are scores of books more or less diverging from the first opinions of Mrs. Eddy, and scores of teachers propagating all sorts of phases of "The Science of Spirit." Inasmuch as this professedly new revelation points to its works of healing as the proofs of its truth, it will be necessary to examine the question of healing generally, if possible to discover if its efficacy lies in any special theories, or in some principle inherent in human nature.

We may at once divide the cures with which the world is familiar into two classes—those which are miraculous and those which are natural. By "miraculous" is meant that the cure was due to the interposition of a higher will, or by the employment of powers which exist, though generally latent, in human beings, doing that which is not done in the ordinary course of nature. We often find it asserted that our Lord did his "mighty works" by those powers which it was intended humanity should possess, whereby the command of God should be carried out, and we should "subdue the earth.' With the fall of man the sceptre of this power fell from our grasp. Occasionally, here and there, a man seemed to have recovered something of it, and our Lord re-possessed it in its fullness, and thereby worked his miracles. No doubt there is some truth in this; but He Himself declared that the Father had given Him works to do. "The Father that dwelleth in Me, He doeth the works"—John xiv., 10. This is a plain statement that certain miracles, which He was then referring to, were done by the higher will interfering with the ordinary course of nature, and this is what we call a miracle. These works are always termed in the Greek "signs." Signs of what? Signs that the doer of them was authorized by a power superior to the ordinary course of nature. That these signs served their purpose Nicodemus is a witness. "No man," said he, "can do the miracles (signs) Thou doest except God be with him." Our Lord Himself appealed to his works in proof of the authority of his teaching: "Believe me for the very works' sake"—John xiv., 11. He endowed his Apostles, in the first instance, with the same capability as He Himself possessed. As the "Christian Scientists" have taken the words of his commission as the motto around their seal, "Heal the Sick, Raise the Dead, Cleanse the Lepers, Cast out Demons," it is advisable to examine more closely this authority. It occurs in the charge given by our Lord to the Twelve Apostles, narrated in Matt. x., 6, etc. He is sending them to the lost sheep of the house of Israel. He forbids them to go into the way of the Gentiles; in order that attention might be gained for their message and their word be delivered with authority, He endues them with power "to heal the sick, cleanse the lepers, raise the dead, cast out demons." It is clear that this power was a special gift for a special purpose, made to special men; and unless it is asserted that the Lord in this "charge" to his chosen twelve intended to address through them all his followers of the centuries to come—an assertion no one would make—it cannot be maintained that we ordinary Christians can draw from these words any authority whatever to "heal the sick."

The only other reference in the Gospels to this power is in the concluding paragraph of S. Mark's Gospel. These would appear to be the very last words our Lord uttered just before his ascension. He is speaking again to his Apostles, and He says: "Go into all the world and preach the Gospel to the whole creation. He that believeth and is baptized shall be saved; but he that believeth not shall be condemned. And these signs shall follow (accompany) them that believe. In my name they shall cast out devils; they shall speak with new tongues; they shall take up serpents; and if they drink any deadly thing it shall in nowise hurt them; they shall lay hands on the sick, and they shall recover."

The unbiased reader will at once conclude that our Lord in this statement did not in any sense declare that it was one of the prerogatives of his followers to be free from sickness, or that it was one of their duties in his name to "heal the sick." These powers are still spoken of as extraordinary; they are still termed "signs;" they stood as witnesses to declare the Divine nature of the message of the Gospel; they were "to accompany those that believed," in order to convince the world that salvation had come. Before the canon of Scripture closed, these signs were exhibited again and again. We have no authorized record of any of the believers drinking without harm a poisoned cup—a common enough mode of murder in those days—but a legend relates how the life of S. John was thus attempted and how he escaped. S. Paul at Melita did shake off the viper, which had fastened on his hand, into the fire and took no harm, and what effect the "sign" had on the islanders S. Luke tells us. And if anyone still needs convincing that these powers were special gifts, not for the benefit of believers themselves, but for the quicker spreading of the Gospel they were charged to propagate, it is conclusively stated by S. Paul in I. Cor. xiv., 22. Referring to the speaking with new tongues, he writes: "Tongues are for a sign not to them that believe, but to them that believe not." That is, the gift was intended to attract the outside world, and give reason, to those who listened, to credit that the Gospel preached was not "of men, but of God." It was, in fact, the very accomplishment of what the Lord had promised, and what S. Mark himself thirty years afterward, with the events before him, stated in the final verse of his narrative: "And they went forth and preached everywhere, the Lord working with them and ratifying the Word by means of accompanying signs." Mark xvi., 20.

That it was never intended that sickness should be banished from our lives, while in this state of probation, but should be used, as all the other disabilities of our present state, for purposes of discipline and means by which we might forge our own characters, is very evident from the teachings of the Word of God.

We are told, and observation amply corroborates the assertion, that the ruler of this world is that evil potentate, that adversary of our souls, the Devil. Our Blessed Lord called him "The Prince of this World." The temptations which waylaid the path of the Lord Himself are always ascribed to his malevolence. At the entrance of his public ministry He is led into the wilderness to be tempted of the Devil. Matt. iv., 1. He is assaulted by temptations which were indicative of all "the contradictions of sinners against Himself." In the natural commiseration of the chief Apostle, when the Lord revealed to them how soon He must suffer, He heard the voice of the Arch-Tempter, and said to Peter: "Get thee behind me, Satan, for thou savourest not the things that be of God, but of men." And when his betrayer, with the wine of the first sacrament upon his lips, went out into the night, to make his proposal to the Sanhedrim, the Evangelist records: "Now Satan having put into the heart of Judas Iscariot to betray him, he went out"—a corroboration of our Lord's own words, that although He had chosen the twelve, one of them was a devil. All through his career He looked upon the opposition He met with and the sorrows which oppressed people as due to "the envy of the devil." Wisdom ii., 24.

To the head and front of the opposition, which finally compassed his death, He said: "Ye are of your father, the devil." In those days spirits of evil gained access to men's souls, and disputed with the man himself the governance of himself. These He "cast out," "suffering them not to speak, for they knew him." He even ascribed to their malevolence those infirmities of the body which elicited his pity. He said of the woman, the curvature of whose spine was such that she "could in nowise straighten herself," that it was Satan who had "bound her, lo! these eighteen years." Luke xiii., 16. Death itself He ascribed to satanic power. "I will forewarn you whom ye shall fear. Fear him who, after he hath killed the body, hath power to cast into hell: yea, I say unto you, fear him." Luke xii., 5.

This terrible view of the condition of our life might be conjectured from the fact that our Lord healed diseases and raised the dead. Because, if the sick were afflicted according to the will of God, and if it was the direct action of the will of God that death should come, how could our Lord have removed the sickness or recalled the dead? He was the only man ever on earth who never ran counter to the will of God, and in that He did deliver the sick and the dead it is a proof that they were not smitten according to the will of God. It is, of course, true that no sparrow can fall to the ground without His high behest, but He allows the power of evil to act within certain limits, that we may have that very discipline by which and through which we gain our liberty.

A pertinent illustration of the relationship which the Almighty Father is pleased to maintain with the Prince of Evil is given to us in the matter of that "infirmity of the flesh" which S. Paul describes as "a messenger of Satan, sent to buffet him." It was so poignant an affliction that the Apostle does not style it "a thorn in the flesh," but "a stake in the flesh." The iron entered into his soul, and to all appearance woefully restrained his usefulness.

Now, S. Paul had in a pre-eminent degree the gift of healing. So full was he of "virtue," that handkerchiefs and aprons which had touched his body conveyed the healing property to the sick and made them well— Acts xix., 11. But the great Apostle had a serious view of the use of sickness, and so reverently did he regard it that he declined to restore his damaged eyesight— for this, no doubt, was his infirmity—himself. He therefore tells his Corinthian converts, that he besought the Lord thrice—II. Cor. xii., 7-10—to heal his sickness, but the Divine assurance was, that it was better for him to bear its burden; that grace was vouchsafed him to carry that cross. "My grace is sufficient for thee," was the reply. Now, in this case, it is unequivocally stated that his diseased eyes were due to satanic power, that this was permitted by the Lord, who could have removed the infirmity, in view of certain contingencies which might happen, and which would be sadly detrimental to S. Paul himself. Some of these he himself perceived. He tells us that this affliction was allowed to keep him humble, lest he "should be exalted above measure" because of "the abundance of the revelations" which had been vouchsafed to him. Lest that pride, which haunts us like our shadow, should arise within him and debase his character, it was necessary, even for him, that his weakness and dependence should be continually forced upon him. Looking at the circumstances from our more distant point of view, we can see many more advantages which accrued from his sickness. The Galatian Church never would have been founded, Gal. iv., 13; we never should have had the Epistle to that Church; the intimacy between S. Paul and S. Luke would never have existed; and probably, therefore, we owe to the Apostle's sickness the Gospel of S. Luke and the Acts of the Apostles; and who shall say that the profundity of the Epistle to the Romans, the depth and energy of the Apostle's thought, are not to be ascribed to the fact that he was often obliged to sit in the dark, and being ever, more or less, denied the wide sight of the outer world, was compelled to turn the eye of his mind in introspective view; and so learned to commune with himself. It was good for S. Paul, as it was for David, that he was afflicted.

Before leaving the pages of the Book of Revelation and examining the power of healing as illustrated in secular history, we must refer to an example of the fact that it is possible for the determined human will to gain its desire, even although the answer to the prayer has not the Divine approval.

It is quite possible, even probable, that S. Paul could have healed himself, without applying to the Divine Counsellor. S. James leads us to conclude that the famine in Israel and the demonstration on Mount Carmel were the result of the stalwart faith of Elijah, "a man of like passions as we are." Not only did no good result come from his bringing force to bear upon the multitude, but at Horeb God Himself taught his faithful servant that "it was not by might, nor by power, but by my spirit," saith the Lord, that men's minds and hearts are influenced. The wind, the fire, the earthquake, had no effect on the prophet himself. It was "the still small voice" of a present personality which bowed him down; and then the command came to him to cease to attempt to move masses, but to deal personally with individuals—Jehu, Hazael, Elisha.

God has been pleased to place great honor on the human will. To it has He committed the reception of the gift of eternal life. With such puissance has He invested it, that in its prerogative has He placed the possession or the non-possession of the Holy Ghost, the Lord and Life Giver. The will of man can withstand the omnipotence of Almighty God. Even the Lord of Lords cannot enter in and take possession of a man's heart unless the will of the man open unto Him. It is, therefore, not a thing to be wondered at that, in deference to the will He Himself has so honored, God does sometimes acquiesce in that the consequences of which we cannot call good. In other words, it is quite within the capability of men to throw down the crosses He has apportioned for them to bear, and rid themselves, by sheer force of will or wealth of resource, of those disabilities which, if borne with patience, would have worked out for them an eternal weight of glory. Of this we have a striking example given us in the history of Hezekiah.

After a life of faithfulness, and brilliant with many signal instances of the favor of the Lord, the great Prophet Isaiah is sent with a message to the king: "Set thine house in order, for thou shalt die and not live." Had Hezekiah received this direct word from God as a wonderful assurance of his eternal safety, had he counted himself well rid of this naughty world and now certain of passing into Abraham's bosom, had he received the summons joyfully and committed his soul unto God as unto a faithful creator, he would have departed in peace. But instead of this, he "turned his face to the wall and wept sore," and in an agony prayed that God would spare his life and lengthen his days. While still on his way, "in the midst of the city," before he had reached his own house, Isaiah is commanded to return to the palace to announce to the king that his prayer was granted, and that God would add fifteen years to his life. Perhaps we may venture to think that the Lord, who "trieth the heart," knew that the discipline of life had done what it could for Hezekiah's character, and that there were, in the future, occasions of temptation likely to arise under whose strain his faith would give way, so that it would be better for him to be "taken from the evil to come." Isaiah, lvii., 1. It is significant that the trial of his faith, in believing the truth of the reprieve, was remarkably shortened, "On the third day thou shalt go up unto the house of the Lord;" and wonderfully supported by a sign from heaven, the Lord "brought the shadow ten degrees backward, by which it had gone down in the dial of Ahaz." II. Kings xx., 11.

In a very short time the weak place in his character was exposed. The writer of the Chronicles tells us that "Hezekiah rendered not again according to the benefit done unto him, for his heart was lifted up." It was the natural rebound from the ever-present thought of that fifteenth year. He said in his thanksgiving prayer for his recovery: "I shall go softly all my years, in the bitterness of my soul." Isaiah xxxviii., 15. He was not the sort of man who could brace his spirit to watch the sure approach of death, not only with calmness, but with triumph. The fear of death had evidently great terror for him. Therefore, by every device, he thrust from the sight of his mind the unwelcome thought. This constant attitude induced a sort of braggadocio, a devil-may-care temperament, which is the other alternative in the face of a great danger. Under such a pressure a man is either softened or hardened. That Hezekiah might know himself it was that Berodach-baladan, King of Babylon, was instigated to send to

Jerusalem an embasage of princes, bearing congratulations and a present. The ancient chronicler puts it with graphic insight: "Howbeit in the business of the ambassadors of the princes of Babylon, who sent unto him to enquire of the wonder that was done in the land, God left him to try him, that He might know all that was in his heart." II. Chronicles xxxii., 31.

It is certainly a corroboration of this narrative that Herodotus found that during the 11,000 years in which the Egyptian priests said they had kept meteorological records, they had noted that the sun had twice gone backwards, which agrees with the two occasions mentioned in the Old Testament.

It is clear that the king was not alone in his proud attitude, but his court, and indeed the whole city, put on airs. To give their visitors the impression that they were a rich and mighty people they displayed all their valuables and dilated on the great sign, to intimate that even the very sun in heaven attended to their wishes; and in consequence we read that "the wrath of the Lord came upon him and upon Judah and Jerusalem." Not only might they have escaped this calamity had their king been safe in Paradise, but another serious event would never have come to pass. In the third year after his recovery his son Manasseh was born. The fifteenth year duly arrived, Hezekiah died, and Manasseh, at the age of twelve, succeeded him. He reigned fifty-five years. There was no species of wickedness he did not revel in. He built altars to the host of heaven in the very courts of the temple of the Lord. "He made his son pass through the fire and observed times and used enchantments and dealt with familiar spirits and wizards; he wrought much wickedness in the sight of the Lord to provoke Him to anger; . . . he seduced them to do more evil than did the nations whom the Lord destroyed before the children of Israel. Moreover, Manasseh shed innocent blood very much, till he had filled Jerusalem from one end to another." Can we wonder that the Lord said He would bring "such evil upon Jerusalem and Judah that whosoever heareth of it, both his ears shall tingle"?—II. Kings xxi., 16. And all this came upon them in natural sequence, because a man would be rid of sickness and would not acquiesce in the will of the Lord, that it was time for him to die.

Every student of Christianity can cite instances where the purely human will demanded of God the recovery of some loved one, and the prayer, to their bitter regret, was granted. Out of many with which I am personally cognizant I cite one.

Some connections of my own, wealthy people, lived at Sydenham, near London. No children had fallen to the household for several years, when a baby boy was born, and appropriately christened Benjamin. When two years old little Bennie was seized with meningitis. The most eminent of the London physicians were summoned, consultation after consultation was held, but it was evident, even to the non-medical eye, that the child must die, and this was the verdict. An eminent ecclesiastic, now gone to his rest, told me he was in the room. He saw the mother, a woman of great piety, open the large Bible on the table, and finding the Lord's promise in Mark xi., 24, "What things soever ye desire, when ye pray, believe that ye receive them, and ye shall have them," kneeling down, she placed her finger on the verse, and, to use his own words, "The room literally shook with the vigor of her demand for the life of her boy."

Her prayer was answered; the child did not die. But he remained in the condition in which the disease had been arrested sixteen years! For sixteen years he lay, a baby in his cradle, and the intimates of the household used to go into the nursery to see "little Bennie." It was said he recognized his mother, but gave no other sign of intelligence. At the end of those long sixteen years the mother was glad and thankful to have him go to the Father's home!

It has ever appeared to reasonable people a strange thing to deny to the God above us that power which we ourselves possess. We can arrest the processes of nature, and by our will interfere with what appear universal laws. We walk upright, defiant of the law of gravity. Then why should not either God's will, if so He deem fit, or even man's will, if so capable, avert in certain cases what appear to be sure consequences? After all, is it not merely the superimposition of a higher and more potent force?

The cure of sickness is lawful if the heart be in willing subservience to the mind of God. We have seen how dangerous it is to heal the sick without reference to Him who alone knows what is in us and what lies before us. Few people can doubt that the power of will to hold us in health is one of the means God has placed at our disposal to enable us to deal with the difficulties of life. But, like all other powers, it is intrusted to us to use only for his service and in his honor.

But to say that man's mission is to sweep out of his path every disability, and that he has commission from the Master to everywhere "heal the sick," is a dangerous doctrine, and subversive of the very occasion of our life. And its contradiction is positive, by the failure in the majority of cases where it is attempted by those who are so deluded as to believe it.

CHAPTER II.

ON HEALING.

IT has naturally been the desire of every generation to heal its sick. Sickness is not a pleasant experience, and, as it not seldom leads to death, the sympathies of the sick as well as those of their immediate friends are keenly awakened, one and all, from every consideration, are filled with anxiety to see the sick one cured.

Nothing makes us realize the weakness of the human arm more than an attack of sickness. The disease holds its way, as a giant striding amongst pigmies. Is it any wonder, then, that in every generation men have obeyed the worshipping instinct of our nature and appealed to the unseen power?

The wealth of the temples of the ancient world was chiefly from votive offerings of those who believed the god had cured them or theirs, of some ill to which flesh is heir. Evidence could be gleaned from every classic writer of sacred places famed in his time for the healing properties they possessed.

Strabo records the marvelous reputation gained in his day by a temple of the Egyptian god, Serapis, which was situated at Canopus, and was reached from Alexandria by canal. He says that eminent persons from all parts of the world congregated there to be healed; that so great was the number of pilgrims that the canal was filled with boats going and returning.

There never was a shrine or holy well that had not tales to tell of, and usually an assortment of crutches and sticks to witness to, the cures performed by its relic or its holy water.

In our day we have the truly wonderful sights at Lourdes. A peasant girl declared the Blessed Virgin had appeared to her. Her story was credited by some, disbelieved by others. People went to see the girl and the place, cures began to be effected, and now there is a splendid church and its accompaniments; and every year not only are great pilgrimages organized, but "The White Train" passes through France and collects on its way one thousand incurables, who are attended by devotees of the highest rank. Out of these one thousand, two hundred are cured. There is no chicanery about this. A committee of medical men of all shades of opinions and beliefs examine these cases before and after the use of the water, and in numberless instances have expressed themselves satisfied of the genuineness of the cure.

But does anybody believe that such cures establish the reality of the existence of the gods of ancient mythology? Or the genuineness of the relics of the saints? Or that the Blessed Virgin really did appear to the French peasant girl? Whatever the power of the cure may be, it is evident that in these cases it resided in the subjects themselves, and not in the object of veneration. It was subjective, and not objective.

Before we attempt to illustrate the effect that the mind has over our bodies, we must notice the case of a healing power which is possessed by some persons. S. Paul distinctly tells us that there is "a gift of healing." Our Blessed Lord had it in its fullness. "The whole multitude sought to touch Him; for there went virtue out of Him and healed them all"—Luke vii., 19; and when the woman in the crowd touched the hem of his garment, unknown to Him, He immediately was cognizant of the craving touch, for He said: "I perceive that virtue has gone out of me." How far the Lord and his Apostles were endued with this gift, and how far their works were the offspring of "power from on high," it is impossible to say. But there is no doubt whatever that, apart from religious belief, or at least independent of it, many persons have a force which is strengthening and health-giving. There are clergymen of whom it is said that the sick infants they baptize almost invariably recover, and everyone knows of persons whose presence in the sick-room is welcomed, and who, by a touch or stroke of the hand, seem to revive the invalid. It is the habit to ascribe to imagination, if not to imposition, the healings of men who in every generation have gained celebrity for the cures they have wrought; therefore there is little disposition to seriously examine their claims.

Francis Schlatter is a case in point. In the fall of last year he attracted in this city of Denver thousands of persons, who passed before him for eight or ten hours every day. Whatever may have been his own religious belief, he made no exaction on the faith of others, and of some of the cures he wrought it must be admitted that the curative power came from him, and was not excited in the patient. Let three cases which came under my own observation suffice:

The cook of one of our oldest residents, in lifting a piano eight years ago, ruptured herself. She suffered many things of many physicians, and was not cured. Often she was unable to work, and although, of course, she wore a truss, was frequently in great pain. Moreover, her eyesight became impaired. She could not see to thread a needle, and could not even sew by gaslight. The second day Schlatter was here she was in the long line which approached him. She is a Swede, and, after the manner of her countrywomen, very taciturn. She never spoke to him, nor he to her. She heard what he said to others. He held her hand. She said as he did so she felt she was cured.

On returning home she took off her truss. I saw her six weeks afterward, and again in six months To use her own words, she said she was "a well woman." Moreover, her eyes regained their wonted strength. She remained apparently in perfect health; at least, she did her work without interruption, her mistress tells me, until a little time ago she left to revisit her native land.

Schlatter never would receive any remuneration, although it was said as much as $500 was offered him in one fee.

Now, contrast this with a parallel case. A lady in my congregation is afflicted in the same way. Finding she was not cured by ordinary treatment, she was persuaded to consult a "Christian Science" healer. This person, after many treatments, assured her she was cured—indeed, that "the pain, the lump, the discomfort, were all the illusions of 'mortal mind,' and had no real existence; she might go home and discard her truss." Which she foolishly did, and was only saved next day by prolonged medical effort from having to undergo the operation for strangulated hernia. She had paid the "scientist" $50.

Another precisely similar case occurred with another lady of my congregation. She consulted a "healer," who treated her every day for six weeks. On leaving for Florida, the "Christian Scientist" proposed to give her "absent treatments" at the same rate of charge. But when on the train, at one of the "set times," she, too, was on the point of desperate trouble. The movements consequent on travel had, of course, brought down the hernia, and it became strangulated, and it was only "reduced" at the cost of great suffering.

But to return to Schlatter, to show that healings are possible without any dependence on any theory whatever. I know a boy of ten, who had hip disease for more than two years before Schlatter came. The disease so increased that the poor little fellow could only lie on the floor on his right side, so propped by pillows that he could not turn over in his sleep. He went to the healer, who told him that in two months it was God's will that he should be well, and from that time he began rapidly to amend. A large lump gathered, but painlessly. It then broke, freely discharged, and then the place permanently healed. The boy has abandoned his crutches, and his leg, though of course deformed, has no sign of disease about it; and it is a year since the "healer" was here.

A third and last case is that of a young man I have known ten years. His digestion was so feeble that at length even the milk and bread he was reduced to live upon, had to be removed by the stomach pump whenever he was seized with a species of convulsion, which he well described as "the blind staggers." His father being the manager of one of our chief daily papers, and his mother most active in all charitable undertakings, he had every medical attention, and in spite of all endeavors he gradually neared his grave. I often saw him, and he was a cause of great anxiety to us all. He went to see Schlatter, and from that hour he began to amend. In a few weeks he could eat anything; his whole system seemed changed. So thankful was he that he became Schlatter's attendant, and held the handkerchiefs and cloths brought to be blessed. Schlatter pressed them between his hands for a few minutes, and many persons whom I have questioned declared that when applied to the body they reddened and drew the skin as a mustard plaster would. When I first heard this I derided the idea, or conceived it to be another illustration of the power of mind over body. But both my young friend and his mother have many evidences to give, which it is difficult to gainsay, as to the singular effect which they both experienced themselves and witnessed on the persons of other people when these "blessed" cloths were applied.

The general opinion of those who were intimately concerned with this singular man is that five per cent.

of those who sought his aid were materially benefited. He himself ascribed the cures to faith in God, which he continually urged. His appearance, very spiritual and distrait, greatly assisted the earnestness of his appeal, and no doubt largely contributed to the effect.

In the "British and Foreign Medical Review," January, 1847, is given a series of cases communicated by a naval surgeon of long standing. This illustration of the astonishing effect of mind over body will render credible the above instance of Schlatter's success:

"A very intelligent officer had suffered for some years from violent attacks of cramps in the stomach. He had tried almost all the remedies usually recommended for the relief of this distressing affection, and for a short period prior to coming under my care the trisnitrate of bismuth had been attended with the best results. The attacks came on about once in three weeks, or from that to a month, unless when any unusual exposure brought them on more frequently. As the bismuth had been useful it, of course, was continued; but notwithstanding that it was increased to the largest dose that its poisonous qualities would justify, it soon lost its effect. Sedatives were again applied to; but the relief afforded by these was only partial, while their effect on the general system was very prejudicial. On one occasion, while greatly suffering from the effect of some preparation of opium, given for the relief of these spasms, he was told that on the next attack he would be put under a medicine which was generally believed to be most effective, but which was rarely used because of its dangerous qualities; but that, notwithstanding these, it would be tried, provided he gave his assent. This he did willingly. Accordingly, on the first attack after this, a powder containing four grains of *ground biscuit* was administered every seven minutes, while the greatest anxiety was expressed (within the hearing of the patient) lest too much should be given.

"The fourth dose caused an entire cessation of pain. Half-drachm doses of bismuth had never procured the same relief in less than three hours. For four successive times did the same kind of attack recur, and four times it was met by exactly the same remedy with like success. After this he joined another ship."

CHAPTER III.

MIND AND MATTER.

TURNING now to the control the mind has over the body, we have within our reach a mass of evidence which goes far to prove, that, *thought of any given bodily change tends to the actual production in the body of the change that thought suggests.*

This statement need not give us any great surprise, if we consider that the body must be secreted by the soul, if by soul we mean the human vitality bequeathed to us by our parents.

Unless we are prepared to admit that the soul gathers to itself and places in their proper position particles of matter, thus building for itself an organism for its own habitation and for the transaction of its business in this material world, unless we admit that the soul thus constructs the body, how are we to account for that family likeness which strangely blends the characteristics of both father and mother? The soul must have a form, and surely it is not beyond our right to presume that, when disembodied, we shall still retain our present appearance? We cannot admit that the body gives form to the soul. It is evident that the soul determines the form of the body, and, if so, then it is no wonder that the alteration of the soul intimately affects the body. That it does so is beyond question. Even after the body has attained its full growth and the appearance of the face has become fixed, let a change occur in the nature of the man—let him become spiritually minded, or even let him have his intelligence stimulated, and everyone will mark his altered appearance. We say he is a changed man.

It is not a mere alteration of muscular setting of which the mind is capable. It will cause actual change in the fabric of the body. A fright has been known to whiten the hair; a feeling will blanch or will redden the face; let anyone concentrate his thought on the tip of any of his fingers, and it will begin to tingle, because the blood is being drawn to that spot. This important fact was noted by no less a medical authority than John Hunter. He writes: "I am confident that I can fix my attention to any part until I have a sensation in that part." Anxiety will take away appetite, which means that those juices essential to digestion are arrested, and the stomach, unprepared to receive food, intimates its disinclination for it. On the other hand, a happy, buoyant spirit is at once the cause and the effect of a good digestion.

But there is a class of evidence which is more inexplicable. Who of us has not in childhood had our warts charmed away? The modus operandi of the charmer was always to make the occasion very solemn; then the mind was adroitly drawn to the obtrusive wart; it was to be rubbed with half an onion, whose other moiety was to be buried in the churchyard exactly one hour after sunset, or some other mysterious treatment was prescribed, and the with the assurance that the wart would disappear that day fortnight, the patient was dismissed; but the mind had been riveted on that wart, and its effect was to banish the intruder; and, what is more curious, no one seems to have noticed the decay of the wart, but suddenly it was found gone!

On this curious, but very suggestive experience, we have a narrative by no less a person than my Lord Chancellor Bacon. "I had from childhood," he says, "a wart upon one of my fingers; afterwards, when I was about sixteen years old, being then in Paris, there grew upon both my hands a number of warts, at the least a hundred, in a month's space. The English Ambassador's lady, who was a woman far from superstitious, told me one day she would help me away with my warts; whereupon she got a piece of lard, with the skin on, and rubbed the warts all over with the fat side, and among the rest that wart I had had from my childhood; then she nailed the piece of lard, with the fat towards the sun, upon a post of her chamber window, which was to the south. The success was that within five weeks' space all the warts went away, and that wart I had so long endured for company. But at the rest I did little marvel, because they came in a short time and might go away in a short time again; but the going away of that which had stayed so long doth yet stick with me."

It is very venturesome to suggest to such a man that he had forgotten anything, but no doubt the Ambassador's lady told him that as the sun melted the lard so would the warts disappear! The boy's mind was by many circumstances fixed on the warts, the grand lady, the foreign city, the bit of lard, and not improbably the evident association between lard and Bacon. The " suggestion " worked, and the warts vanished !

In the time of the Stuarts, " touching for the 'King's Evil'" was one of the regular duties of the king. There must have been numerous cases where the scrofula was actually removed, not by the touch of the king's finger, but by the effect of the powerfully directed mind to the affected gland.

There are on record some ninety cases of the stigmata, the marks of the nails and the spear-thrust in our Lord's body, appearing on persons deeply religious. Many of these cases are established beyond question.

S. Francis Assissi, the founder of the Franciscan Order of monks, was the first in whom the stigmata were said to be visible, both before and after his death.

In the next century, the fourteenth, the rival order, the Dominicans, gloried in the exhibition by S. Catherine of Sienna of the same marks; but there must have been some doubts as to the reality of the appearances, for in 1475 Pope Sixtus IV. published a bull ordering the erasure of the stigmata from all the pictures of S. Catherine. But, despite the infallibility of the Pope, this may not be taken as conclusive evidence that this hysterical girl of twenty-three had not the stigmata. The rivalry between the Franciscans and Dominicans was something indescribable, and it is quite possible the bull of the Pope did not altogether turn on the cogency of the evidence.

If later years had not supplied us with unquestionable instances of marks on the skin coming at the instigation of the will, abnormally directed, we might be inclined to believe that the origin of the stigmata in every case might be naturally accounted for, and not seldom be traced to the act of the persons themselves. Hysterical patients are singularly adroit, and will inflict wounds upon themselves to induce that sympathy for which they crave with more desperate yearning than the toper for his dram.

An hysterical girl once confessed to me that she herself had thrust a needle down to the bone in her arm, in order that a doctor, she had leanings to, might cut it out, and the rest of us have our sympathy excited. This girl could cause hemorrhages when she chose, and completely deceived some of our best physicians. When she lost the power she used carmine dye, and was of course discovered.

The reader is referred to the article on "Stigmatization" in the Encyclopædia Britannica, where is given the case of Louise Lateau, a peasant girl in Hainault, upon whom the stigmata appeared in 1868. Her case was investigated by Professor Lefebvre, of Louvain, who was for fifteen years the physician of two lunatic asylums, and therefore not likely to be deceived by an hysterical girl, and he wrote an account of the phenomenon, which was published at Louvain in 1870.

We have lately had revived interest in hypnotism, the modern name for mesmerism. Many surgical operations have been performed on favorable subjects without pain when mesmerized. This is by no means improbable, because it is evident that by mesmerism the mind of the subject is diverted from the ordinary channel of its operations, and by that curious control, at present called "suggestion," is so intently fixed elsewhere that it gives no heed to ordinary demands on its attention. That such a mental condition is perfectly possible is amply proved by the well-authenticated instances of soldiers being wounded during the awful excitement of a battle, and never being conscious of the pain which the passage of the bullet must have caused, only discovering the wound after the action.

This peculiar mental phenomenon is the true explanation of many of the cures of "Christian Science." Mrs. Eddy, being quite aware that mesmerism was a powerful rival to her claims, is unmeasured in her denunciation of it. Here is one, out of many, of her onslaughts, that is so palpably the writing of a frightened woman that it is impossible to restrain a smile to see her volubly denounce and yet at once admit the potency of her rival:

> Mesmerism is the right hand of Humbug, and is either delusion or fraud. When first teaching mental science I permitted students to manipulate the head, ignorant that this could harm or hinder the spiritual direction of thought. . . . By thorough examination I learned that manipulation hinders, instead of helps, mental healing. It establishes a mesmeric connection between patient and practitioner, and so gives the latter more opportunity to influence the thoughts and actions of the former in whatever direction he may choose, and sometimes with error instead of truth. . . . . Mesmeric influence is not confined to manipulation, but is employed variously, and becomes the subtle agent of the worst crimes that mortals can commit.—"Science and Health," pp. 197-415, 74th Edition.

This is a real and dreadful power to reside in "the right hand of Humbug!" This is no "imaginary power."

But if mesmerism can produce an actual alteration of the skin, it can also cause material changes in unseen organs, and put right that which has become disordered.

In the proceedings of the Society for Psychical Research, vol. vii., p. 339, quoted in a late number of the "Popular Science Monthly" by Professor Newbold, there are related several cases in which medical men, by means of mesmeric suggestion, caused upon the persons of their subjects marks and crosses to appear and disappear at stated times. One of them, Dr. Biggs, mesmerized his housemaid, and said to her: "Now, listen attentively; a cross is going to appear on your right forearm and remain there until I tell it to go away. Here is where it is to appear." He then marked a cross with his forefinger on the inner side of her right forearm. "Have you understood what I said to you?" The mesmerized girl replied, "Yes." He then awakened her. For the next two or three days she seemed sulky and out of sorts, and would now and then rub her arm where the cross was to appear. She said she did so because there was an itching, although there was as yet no appearance of irritation. He then mesmerized her again and asked, "Do you recollect what I told you the other day about the cross that is to appear on your forearm?" "Yes." "Will it appear?" "Yes." "When?" "In a few days." "Well, it must come out in three days. Do you understand me?" "Yes." By the time appointed a dusky red cross made its appearance. Never a word had been said to her about the cross in her waking moments, and she kept it as much as possible out of sight, but the end of it could be occasionally seen below her sleeve. It was often examined by putting her to sleep. Seeing it one day the doctor said, "Why, Maria, what is the matter with your arm? Have you hurt it? What mark is this? Let me see. Pull up your sleeve." She did so, with a slightly sulky, ashamed air. "Why, it looks like a cross. Where did you get this?" "I don't know, sir." "How long has this been on your arm?" "More than a month, sir." "Have you felt anything?" "No, sir; only at one time I had a great deal of itching and burning, and a few days afterwards this mark came on my arm." The cross continued many months after she had left the doctor's service, and it only disappeared upon her calling on her late master to remove it, which he did by mesmerizing her and telling her, while asleep, that the cross would disappear in a few days, which it did.

This capability of the mind, in the peculiar hypnotic state, of producing an actual alteration of the flesh is no doubt the explanation of the appearance of the stigmata. These persons, usually girls, of the ninety cases recorded by Roman Catholic authorities seventy-two were females and only eighteen males, became by the contemplation of the crucifix mesmerized. The one great idea upon their minds, before they went into the hypnotic condition, was the wounds of the Crucified One. The seclusion of their lives; the one topic of their conversation; their environment, all contributed to direct and impress the thought. The pardonable anxiety to be so honored as "to bear in the body the marks of the Lord Jesus," not a little stimulated by the notoriety which the event would secure for themselves and their community, all tended to subscribe the conditions essential for the effect, and so it came to pass.

The modus operandi of the "Christian Scientist" healer is to all intents and purposes that of the hypnotist. By the silence, the motionless sitting, the subdued voice, the cabalistic sentences—for they are senseless, and cannot excite the intelligence—the mind is soothed; then the suggestion is given, and in the denial of disease the repeated assertion of particular cure is pointedly made and impressed; thus directed, the mind exercises its power, all too little used, of stimulating nerval action, and so inducing in the tissues the change which the thought desires. This is probably the explanation of these cures.

This widespread belief seems to be the rebound of the mind of humanity from that abject materialism the first heralds of awakening science sought, half a century ago, to impose upon us. It is possible to gain a hearing now, for the effect of the unseen, and to believe that there are causes of visible results which lie beyond the pale of the tangible. Publications which only a few years ago would have refused to notice any account of cures beyond the limits of what they termed medical science, do so no longer.

The "British Medical Journal" of November 16, 1895, contains this account of a cure beyond the explanation of the profession:

"A 'miraculous' cure has recently occurred in Moscow, where it has caused considerable excitement. It is, perhaps, a more than usually interesting instance, and therefore deserving of the permanent record given to it by Professor Kozhevnikoff. . . . The patient was a lecturer in the Moscow University.

He had suffered from a severe form of sycosis menti, (eruption of the hair follicles on the chin) since June, 1894. He had visited Vienna, Berlin, Buda-Pesth, Kieff, and other places, seeking the best advice. In April last he returned to Moscow. His chin was then covered with a freshly suppurating eruption. He now sought the advice of a 'wise woman,' who was an attendant at the baths, and was in the habit of giving herbs and 'simples' to her clients. In this case no such remedy was employed. He was told to meet the woman next morning at five o'clock in the Temple of the Saviour, the colossal church on the Moskva River, which has been building all the century and is yet incomplete, in memory of the famous events of 1812. He came as told, and while he remained a passive onlooker the woman prayed for three or four minutes. The same thing was repeated that evening, and again the following morning. But in the meantime the eruption on his face had begun to improve; the discharge ceased, the swelling subsided, and in twenty-four hours scarcely a sign of the disease was left. Such are the facts as given by the patient himself, and confirmed by Professor Kozhevnikoff."

Some other details were added, showing that the patient was of an impressionable, perhaps hysterical temperament; that the woman used a cabalistic prayer, which she would not reveal. The time, the surroundings were all favorable, and the result was, no doubt, due to the power of the mind, when properly directed, upon a body in a recipient condition.

This "force" is far more frequently put into use than is recognized. Dr. Carpenter, in his "Nature and Man," has this paragraph: "Every medical man of large experience is well aware how strongly the patient's undoubting faith in the efficacy of a particular remedy or mode of treatment assists its action; and when the doctor is himself animated by such a faith he has the more power of exciting it in others. A simple prediction, without any remedial measure, will sometimes work its own fulfillment. Thus Sir James Paget tells of a case in which he strongly impressed upon a woman, having a sluggish, non-malignant tumor in the breast, that this tumor would disperse within a month or six weeks; and so it did. He perceived this patient's nature to be one on which the assurance would act favorably, and no one could more earnestly and effectively enforce it. On the other hand, a fixed belief on the part of the patient that a mortal disease has seized upon the frame, or that a particular operation or system of treatment will prove unsuccessful, seems in numerous instances to have been the real occasion of fatal result."

The mere presence of some medical men has a far more curative effect than their prescriptions, because of the impetus their strong personality gives to the will of the patient, which beneficially reacts upon that ever ready disposition of nature to repair damage and restore to their proper working any disordered functions.

The cases thus far cited are all of a kind which it is conceivable that nerval energy might control. The rupture of the Swedish cook may have been partially mended by nature, for three membranes must be torn before the actual rupture occurs, and the impetus given to her nervous force by the expectation engendered by her contact with the healer and his surroundings may have greatly strengthened and accelerated the healing process.

The recovery of the use of her eyesight is to be certainly ascribed to the same cause. We hear sometimes of persons being cured by this class of healers of loss of sight. "The blind receive their sight!" has often been the exulting cry of "Christian Scientists" when lauding their cult as a new revelation. Many apparent diseases of the eye are due to lapse of nerval force. If we all lived long enough we should probably all suffer from cataract, which is the clouding of the crystalline lens. If the life has its full vigor, the secretions which form that lens are transparent, but if the controlling force becomes enfeebled, then the deposited material is not clear, the lens gradually becomes opaque, and we say a cataract is formed. There is no evidence, however, that the opaque lens ever has become again clear. But sometimes the opaqueness may occur in the cornea, the clear material which glazes the pupil. This, by an unskilled doctor, is frequently confounded with cataract, and this cloudiness does become clear again by invigorating the constitution. It is quite possible, therefore, to conceive this ailment being removed by the impetus imparted by an awakened will, under the application of the methods of "Christian Science," or other similar modes of treatment. So it is of deafness. All the apparatus of hearing may be in perfect condition, but if the nerves are lazy and decline to carry the impressions from the ear to the brain, nothing is heard, and the person is deaf. But now let some impetus be supplied to the flow of nerval force, and the deaf hear!

The same sort of consideration may be applied to rheumatism and dyspepsia, and many of those ailments from which women suffer. In all these cases there is no actual change in the construction of the muscles or organs, but their normal action is impeded either by the lack of some necessary secretion, or, as in the case of rheumatism, by the want of the removal of effete matter. In such cases willpower and nerval stimulants may remove the disability and restore to health. We may call it nerval force, or will-power, or what we like, but we all know it is a veritable factor in maintaining the perfect working of the body.

Of late years we have learned that many diseases are due to the agency of life. Microbes infest us; they float in the air; they inhabit, in whole colonies, dollar bills; they congregate on our clothing; they are everywhere. Then why is it they do not so find residence in all of us as to produce constant diseases? Several persons are exposed to the same infection. Why is it that only one of the number takes the disease? "Because the others were not susceptible," is the usual answer. This probably is due to their nerval condition at the time. Experience has long shown that in the morning hours, before the work of the day has taxed the nerval energy, infection has less effect. As medical students we were not allowed to visit the fever wards unless quite well, and in the morning. Then, if this be the case, anything which is liable to nerve the constitution and render it braced and terse is likely to reduce to a minimum the possibility of taking disease, and this end is not a little gained by the assurance that there is no disease to contract, and that the possibility of infection does not exist.

But this mental stimulant is by no means a specific; it is only a preventative. And when the microbes have effected a lodgment in that particular gland or locality where is to be found food upon which they can thrive, then it is impossible to conceive how they can be reached and killed. They must live their life, and "bring forth fruit after their kind." Therefore, when "Christian Scientists" and "divine healers," etc., assert they can and have cured, say, cancer, the statement is to be received with the gravest doubt. In my ministerial work I have several times attended to the Valley of the Shadow of Death some who have died of cancer, who gave heed to these "seducing spirits" and yielded themselves to the fallacious teaching of these people, to their great and bitter regret. Their time, their short time, was wasted, and worse; their mind and heart were diverted from holding on to Him who is our only help in time of need; their spiritual sight was beclouded with a haze of impersonality—a comfortless "all mind" or "infinite spirit"—and they found to their desperate sorrow that they had lost sight of Him who alone saith, "Come unto Me, and I will give you rest." "When thou passest through the waters I will be with thee."

There have been also not a few who have brought upon themselves very serious censure. They abandoned the known hope surgery and medical remedies offer, and deliberately consigned those, whom they loved, to a theory which cannot be proved, and, indeed, is continually disproved. Such people ought not to be allowed so to tamper with the sick. In older countries the law protects the helpless from such harmful experiments, by either preventing those who have not secured proper diplomas from professing to cure diseases, or else preventing those who have the care of the helpless sick from declining to call in medical assistance.

There are some deluded people in England who call themselves "the peculiar people," whose belief is, that prayer is all that is needed for the recovery of the sick; and there may often be seen in the law reports the account of the trial, and very proper imprisonment, of such persons, the law defending the helpless, and rescuing them from being the subjects of crude and contradictory theories; just as the law there prevents the vivisection of animals in attempts to verify mere guesses, or to substantiate some theory which is ill-considered and contains no probability of being true.

Turning from this class of disease to those ailments caused by an actual displacement in the fabric of the system, we find the numerous sects of 'mind healers' at wide variance of opinion.

Mr. Henry Wood, who poses as the philosopher of the "Christian Science" cult, and with whose every sentence any educated person would be disposed to cavil, either as to its form, or its diction, or the opinion it expresses, roundly declares that when any accident happens which breaks a bone or dislocates a joint, the wise "Christian Scientist" will at once call in medical aid.

Not so, Mrs. Eddy. She is by no means disposed

to allow that "divine man" is in any direction limited.

"Christian Science" (she says, p. 400) is always the most skillful surgeon, but surgery is the branch of its healing which will be last demonstrated. However, it is but just to say that the author has already in her possession well-authenticated records of the cure, by herself and her students, through mental surgery alone, of dislocated joints and spinal vertebræ.

Politeness would forbid us to contradict a lady, but we may venture to question "*the well-authenticated.*" Nothing is more rare than to have "an unvarnished tale," and nothing more difficult than to wipe off the accretions of inaccuracy. If every story of a cured disability was sifted to its source, it would be soon apparent that none of these 'mind healers' ever have or ever will restore to its place a dislocated bone, or mend a fracture.

Dr. Buckley, in the March number of the "Century" for 1887, gives the natural history of one of these stories, and, as it is a sample of all the rest, I quote it. It is thus narrated by the late W. E. Boardman, who says the story was told him by Dr. Cullis. Dr. Gordon has reproduced it in his "Mystery of Healing." It would be difficult to find three better men than these, each of them celebrated for personal piety and for widespread evangelical influence; each of them quite incapable of knowingly varying from the exact truth, and yet see how all three assisted in the production and the continuing of a wholly false account. Here is the story, in the graphic telling of Mr. Boardman, who apparently adopts the language of the father:

"The children were jumping off from a bench, and my little son fell and *broke both bones of his arm below the elbow*. My brother, who is a professor of surgery in the college at Chicago, was here on a visit. I asked him to set and dress the arm. He did so, put it in splints, bandages, and in a sling. The dear child was very patient, and went about without a murmur all that day.

"The next morning he came to me and said, 'Dear papa, please take off these things?' 'Oh, no, my son; you will have to wear these five or six weeks before it will be well.' 'Why, papa, it is well.' 'Oh, no, my dear child, that is impossible.' 'Why, papa, you believe in prayer, don't you?' 'You know I do, my son.' 'Well, last night when I went to bed it hurt me very bad, and I asked Jesus to make it well.'

"I did not like to say a word to chill his faith. A happy thought came. I said, 'My dear child, your uncle put the things on, and if they are taken off he must do it.' Away he went to his uncle, who told him he would have to go as he was six or seven weeks, and must be very patient. When the little fellow told him Jesus had made him well he said, 'Pooh! pooh! nonsense,' and sent him away. The next morning the poor boy came to me and pleaded with so much sincerity and confidence that I more than half believed, and went to my brother and said to him, 'Had you not better undo his arm and let him see for himself? Then he will be satisfied. If you do not, I fear, though he is very obedient, he may be tempted to undo it himself, and then it may be worse for him.' My brother yielded, and took off the bandages and the splints, and exclaimed, 'It is well, absolutely well!' and hastened to the door to keep from fainting."

Now, if this were a narrative under the inspection of "a higher critic," scanning it for signs of genuineness, he would undoubtedly find many.

But the case was thoroughly investigated by Dr. Lloyd, of the University of Pennsylvania, and in "The Medical Record" for March 27, 1886, he published a letter from the very child, now grown up and a physician:

"DEAR SIR:

"The case you cite, when robbed of all its sensational surroundings, is as follows:

"The child was a spoiled youngster, who would have his own way, and when he had a *green stick* fracture of the forearm, and, having had it bandaged for several days, concluded he would much prefer going without a splint. To please the spoiled child the splint was removed, and the arm carefully adjusted in a sling. As a matter of course, the bone soon united, as is customary in children, and, being only partially broken, of course all the sooner. This is the miracle.

"Some nurse, or crank, or religious enthusiast, ignorant of matters physiological and histological, evidently started the story, and unfortunately my name—for I am the party—is being circulated in circles of faith curists, and is given the sort of notoriety I do not crave. . . .

"Very respectfully yours,
"CARL H. REED."

Ex uno disce omnes!

Considering that the discoverer of this beneficent revelation is a woman, and that by far the greater number of its devotees are women, it would be strange, indeed, if that great trial of womanhood, child-birth, were not to be dealt with. On p. 77, in "Science and Health," Mrs. Eddy narrates a painless labor she presided over in Lynn, Mass., in 1874, and then, mirabile dictu! this great and pressing subject is barely mentioned. In the index, indeed, there is not a little reference under "Child-Birth," "Obstetrics," and "Parturition," but most of the page references are the same, and the total result is sadly disappointing. The whole desire of an expectant mother is to avoid pain, and here are all the crumbs of comfort, the high priestess of a cult whose chief profession is to banish pain, herself vouchsafes to her eager listeners. On page 447, under the head of "Obstetrics," we have:

Teacher and students should also be familiar with the obstetrics taught by the science.

With this brave heading we may well imagine many an anxious woman took heart, and with joyous expectation read on, only to find, after yearning for bread, Mrs. Eddy offers a stone!

To attend properly the birth of the new child, or the Divine idea, you should so detach mortal thought from its material conceptions that the birth will be natural and safe.

Then follows some very cautious and mysterious language. Mrs. Eddy takes great care not to promise painlessness in the process, and she is much too adroit to submit the truth of her theories to an experimental test, such as must often and inevitably occur to "Christian Science" women. She therefore lets one of them state a single experience of more than twenty years ago, she herself avoiding any assertion. Surely, during the time her book has been multiplying to one hundred and five editions, thousands have had the opportunity to learn how their theories stood the test of that great trial. By this time the evidence must have become such an accumulated mass as to triumphantly declare the truth of the "Christian Science" theories, if there is any truth whatever in them. But where is it? There is none! or it would have been only too eagerly forthcoming. Mrs. Eddy, in a late edition of her book, evidently is dissatisfied with the testimony of the mothers; her expectations are in the future; this she states in a sentence of curious indefiniteness. If a charlatan, convicted hopelessly of fraud, wants to study a mode of verbiage under which to cover his retreat, I commend him to this clever passage. It is a continuation of what I have just quoted:

> Through gathering new energies, an idea should injure none of its useful surroundings in the travail of spiritual birth. It should not have within it a single element of error, and should remove properly whatever is offensive. Then would the new idea, conceived and born of Truth and Love, be clad in white garments. Its beginning will be meek, its growth sturdy, and its maturity undecaying. When this new birth takes place, the "Christian Science" infant is born of the Spirit, and can cause the mother no more suffering. Thus it will always be when Truth is allowed to fulfill her perfect work!

This is the only utterance of the oracle in response to the most imperative demand of womanhood; here is the one case of all others where the "Christian Science" theory might be expected to be worth something; and what is it? A passage of such clever non-committal as the priests of Delphi themselves might well envy!

Oh! ye disappointed mothers, will not your sufferings teach you to estimate the worth of this delusion, and discard a teaching so utterly at variance with your experiences!

Occasionally the will may reduce the pain; but these theories are not essential to mental determination, and occasionally nature is so sympathetic that the ordeal is passed with scarce inconvenience. The other day, in this neighborhood, a doctor left a woman a happy mother at two o'clock in the morning. He returned at nine, to see if all was right. He took his breakfast at the restaurant which she and her husband kept, and he found that his patient had fried the oysters!

The practice of every medical man will furnish similar instances; and if a votary of "Christian Science" is so spared as to have a painless delivery, then it was a combination of circumstances which favored her, and she owed nothing whatever to Mrs. Eddy or her teachings.

Let anyone consult "The Influence of the Mind Upon the Body," by Dr. Tuke, and he will there find instances of almost every disease being cured by the action of the mind—inflammatory rheumatism, dropsy, and what was apparently a case of far-gone consumption amongst the rest.

There is no evil that does not bring with it some good; and if the delusion of this "Science" works evil to many it may not be wholly useless if only the attention of this generation is turned to the power that mind, rightly directed, may exert over disease.

To sum up, then, the conclusions pointed to by the experiences we have cited. It may be safely held that will-power has a very evident and decided control over the body; that God never intended his people to have immunity from those ills to which flesh is heir; but that sickness is to be treated, as all the other disciplines of life, as a means of spiritual education. The injunction of S. James that the sick might call for the Elders of the Church, and have them anoint the patient with oil and pray for recovery, was never intended as a substitute for medical treatment, but to supply that Godly dependence which was never inculcated by physicians of that day and seldom by their brethren of this generation. The words of Jesus, the Son of Sirach, in Ecclesiasticus xxxviii., express, no doubt, the sentiments of S. Paul and his friend, "the beloved Physician," as the attachment of S. Luke to the great apostle indicates in what light they held the words of S. James: "Honor a physician with the honor due unto him, for the uses ye may have of him: for the Lord hath created him. For of the Most High cometh healing. . . . The Lord hath created medicines out of the earth; and he that is wise will not abhor them. Was not the water made sweet with wood, that the virtue thereof might be known? And He hath given men skill, that He might be honored in his marvellous works. With such doth He heal men and taketh away their pains. . . . My son, in thy sickness be not negligent. But pray unto the Lord, and He will make thee whole. . . . Then give place to the physician, for the Lord hath created him: let him go not from thee, for thou hast need of him. . . . He that sinneth before his Maker let him fall into the hand of the physician"—and let all the people say, Amen.

CHAPTER IV.

"CHRISTIAN SCIENCE" HEALING.

IT is now beginning to be recognized that the human mind is not one uniform and homogeneous machine; it contains wheels within wheels. To the close observer it becomes evident that parts of the mind are capable of almost independent action. It is a common experience with men who are accustomed to speak in public that they are conscious of two currents of thoughts, the lips pronouncing the one, and the other part of the mind preparing for what is to come next, or probably making some observation connected with their audience which shall modify their mode of address. We seem to be arriving at the conclusion that beneath the active surface of the mind there lies an inactive but recipient mental plane, which has been called the 'subjective mind.' This mental department appears to receive involuntarily, whatever impression the senses impart to it, and faithfully to retain them, although what we may call the active and observing department of the mind may make no attempt whatever intelligently to understand, or to retain, the impressions so made.

A very typical instance of this observation is recorded by Mr. Hudson in his "Physic Phenomena," where it is related that a servant girl at Gottingen, in the delirium of typhoid fever, uttered sentences in Greek, Hebrew and Latin on theological subjects. Many of these sentences were written down. The history of the girl was traced by one of the attending physicians; and he found that she had once been in the service of a learned Lutheran pastor, who was in the habit of walking up and down a passage in his house, a door from which opened into the kitchen where the girl was working, and reading aloud from the works of Greek and Latin fathers. The pastor was dead, but he found his sister alive, who still possessed his library; and his painstaking search was rewarded by the discovery, in the favorite authors of the deceased minister, of the actual sentences that the girl had recited in her delirium.

The only way of accounting for this is to suppose that the sounds which fell upon her ear, and could have been of no possible interest to her, were faithfully registered as they had been received, by that part of her mind which has been termed 'subjective;' and during the process of the disease, certain conditions had been arrived at by which the contents of that part of the mind were re-delivered to the organs of speech, and without any mental effort of her own she reproduced, with something of the pomposity of voice in which they had been originally delivered to it, the very sentences, in unknown tongues, which had reached her ears years before.

That this subjective mind does exist, and faithfully retains all the impressions it has received, has frequent evidence in the sudden recollection of a series of events which apparently had been absolutely forgotten. It is a common occurrence with persons on the brink of sudden death, especially if they are drowning, to declare that, with fearful rapidity, the whole of their past lives, even to minute details, passed in rapid panorama before their mental view.

If we admit the existence of this compartment of the mind, we may have some explanation of the facts of hypnotism. A well-known nerval specialist tells me he has successfully treated certain dypsomaniacs by hypnotizing them, and impressing upon their subjective mind the fact that alcohol would make them violently sick, which thereafter it invariably does. One of his patients lately, not having touched strong drink for a year or more, attended a public dinner. Of course he took no wine, but in the sauce for the pudding at the end of the dinner there was some rum; tasting of it, he hurriedly left the table to carry out the "suggestion" made over a year since.

This glimpse into the construction of the mind, and the wonderful capacity of its 'subjective' province, will lend us no little aid in offering some explanation of the numerous cures effected by "Christian Science" and kindred beliefs.

A frequent experience of "Christian Science" healing, which is triumphantly pointed to as proof positive of the truth of the theory, is that a sufferer was healed by the perusal of Mrs. Eddy's book, quite apart from the influence of any healer, or the effect of 'the sympathy of numbers' in a community of "Christian Scientists." The explanation of this effect may not be far to seek.

It must be remembered that, speaking generally,

the ills to which flesh is commonly heir may be divided into two classes. Those which are due to the invasion of the body by foreign life, and those which may be ascribed to disturbed nerval action. Of the former, phthisis, pneumonia, diphtheria, cancer, typhoid, typhus and scarlet fevers, with some other ailments, are now definitely known to be the result of the disturbance due to the invasion of certain localities by microbes. These organisms, which are mostly of a vegetable nature, can be easily seen and recognized under the microscope. Like other orders of life, they have their day and generation. They breed profusely, and exhaust all the nutriment they find in the gland they have invaded. This gland the meanwhile is incapacitated for its normal action, and the whole body, lacking that which the injured gland should supply, is thrown into disturbance. After the marauders have appropriated all they can get, they die for lack of supply; then nature sets to work to repair the damage of the raid, and the patient gradually recovers.

Of the number of the host of the invaders few people have any conception. A young doctor, who is given to this department of his profession, told me the other day that he had caused one of his patients to bring to him the sputa he had expectorated in the morning. By dividing it by weight, and then counting the baccilli under the microscope in a fractional part, he found that in the quantity brought there could not be less than 5,500,000! What must have been the number of the host entrenched in the poor fellow's lungs!

It looks as impossible, as it is improbable, that any

power of mind can kill these invaders directly, yet, unless they can be either destroyed or incapacitated, that disturbance we call fever must continue. This class of diseases have not and cannot be cured by "Christian Science," despite that it is frequently asserted that this is done. But it must be remembered that nerval derangement, or that obstruction to the normal tides of life we call congestion, may frequently give rise to symptoms by which the unskillful eye is deceived, and often the disease is called by the more serious name, when a far less cause of disturbance was really the ailment.

It is high time that State authorities defended the public from the mischief done by "Christian Science" healers, who are wholly ignorant of the causes of the ailments of their 'patients.'

They ought not to be allowed to practice upon any case, unless a medical opinion has first been obtained as to the nature of the disease; and if the invalids are found to be suffering from any of the class of diseases of which we are speaking, they ought to be handed over to properly authorized medical men.

In every community inflicted by this novel cult, cases of life-long remorse can be told, of children with scarlet and typhoid fever, whose lives were in all probability wantonly sacrificed by the preposterous assumption of the healer and the astounding credulity of the parents. These heartbroken people cling to the flimsy theory to which they committed the life of their precious child with an agony of desperation; for if they ever come to doubt it, and discard it, they must accuse themselves of the untimely death of their innocent!

"CHRISTIAN SCIENCE" HEALING. 51

But the second class of ailments, which are chiefly due to nerval derangement, are the legitimate quarry of any set of practitioners who can bring to bear the mind of the sufferer to set to rights the disorder.

Faith curers, mind healers, mesmeric healers, "Divine Scientists," and "Christian Scientists" and company, can none of them do much harm, and often great good, by their various treatments of this class of ailments. If any cure be effected, it has nothing to do with the truth or untruth of the particular theory of the professor; it is simply that by his methods the mind is directed to the trouble, and the normal condition of the body is stimulated to reassert itself. Success greatly, nay, often entirely, depends upon the disposition of the mind of the patient, the nerval susceptibility, and the strength of the expectation. If these be favorable, then a perusal of Mrs. Eddy's book is no small mesmerizing condition. The constant repetition of senseless sentences confuses and benumbs the faculties of the active layer of the mind, in which dwells the intelligence; the 'subjective' mind beneath is strongly impressed with the desired 'wholeness;' and it is the liberation, as it were, of this mental power to see to the repair of the damage, which really causes the cure. The vast mass of those who are relieved are women, and there is a sentence which is constantly being repeated by "Scientists," which really is the confession of their own secret consciousness, and which tells volumes of the causes of their ailments. They assure their votaries that 'sin must be removed,' and after the cure, 'that they must go and sin no more,' which must be to no small number very pertinent advice.

That a mesmeric element enters into the process, I saw curiously illustrated, when one of the lights of the cult in denouncing Mrs. Cramer, the leader of the opposition, "The Divine Healers," declared with the utmost vigor, "She heals by mesmerism—by hypnotism." We easily discern our own faults in others.

We have still to supply some explanation of those cures which are said to have been performed 'by absent treatment;' that is, by the effect of one mind upon another, either near or far off.

All things are possible, but this can only be accepted as fact, after careful investigation of several cases, and as yet I have never seen evidence sufficient to warrant the belief that such cures have been wrought. But if they have, then their explanation must be sought for in the direction of that mental sympathy, and even actual communion of thought, which appears to exist between certain persons, under certain conditions. This chapter would expand to the size of a volume, to recount all the instances within reach which go to prove that there exists a subtle communication between some persons.

A physician tells me he has in his practice a family, consisting now of the father and mother and three children; that when each of these children came into the world the father suffered pains which were synchronous and equally severe as those of the mother!

Dr. Tuke, in his work on the effect of sympathy, narrates the instance of a lady who was greatly attached to a little child. The child, running through a garden-gate towards her, had its ankle caught by the iron gate closing quickly behind it. She felt a sharp pain in her own ankle, and on reaching home found it much swollen, and the mark of the gate, as if it had crushed her own foot and not that of the child. This much must suffice to indicate the closeness of the chain of sympathy which binds some people into almost one. Everybody's experience can furnish numerous similar instances.

That other condition, essential to the theory of 'absent treatment,' the communication of one mind with another, is a much-debated question. But, personally, I am convinced that under advantageous circumstances this, too, is possible. The requisite conditions, however, are so seldom found in conjunction that it almost precludes their general application as an explanation of cure by 'absent treatment.' Still, the conditions do exist, and it is possible that one or two peculiarly advantageous circumstances may have presented themselves, and, under them, cures at a distance may have been wrought; and the fame of these isolated instances have given countenance to a host of dubious relatives, who, if strictly examined, would turn out to be either mistakes or impostures.

Out of many personal instances I shall only state one, itself sufficient to prove the possibility. When an undergraduate, spending my vacation in my father's parish in a Yorkshire dale, there came to the town a conjurer, Signor Barnado, a tall, imposing man, with a black beard. Part of his entertainment was the exhibition of a clairvoyant, who was in the habit of cleverly describing articles given to the conjurer by the audience, or repeating sentences silently recited by him. It was evident that all this could not be done except upon the supposition that she could read his mind. I had a friend, a country gentleman, then at his fishing box, some thirty miles away at the side of a trout stream. I well knew the room he sat in in the evening, and I wrote to him, telling him to be examining his fly-book at 9 o'clock next Tuesday evening. As the hour arrived I stood up in the audience, and said to the conjurer: "I have a friend thirty miles from here. I want to know what he is doing and where he is." Barnado asked me if I knew what he was about; I replied, I did. He put the question to the blindfolded girl, and she began to describe my friend to the life, his fresh face, his blue-spotted silk necktie, his gold spectacles, the mahogany furniture, the green-figured cloth on the table, the fluted silver candlesticks; he was reading a book. "What is it about?" asked Barnado. "I do not know," said the girl. "Turn to the title-page and read it." "There is no title-page." Then suddenly, after a short pause, she said, "It's about fly-fishing."

"Now," I said, "what is the name of the village?" Barnado asked me if I would tell him, and he would stand near me, and away from the platform, but I replied that I preferred not to do so. He then asked the girl if she could tell, and after a moment or two she rightly replied, "Pateley Bridge."

As this very interesting episode was in progress, I found she was reading my mind. As I arranged the furniture of the room, so she did; as I pictured the fluted silver candlesticks, so exactly she described them; and if I had put on the end of my tongue that my friend was fishing at Timbuctoo, she would have said so.

"CHRISTIAN SCIENCE" HEALING.

I have always been thankful I had this experience when I was a young man. For by its revelation I have laid to rest the perturbed mind of many and many a person, greatly disturbed by the pretended revelation of some spiritualistic medium.

The 'communications' made by these people are entirely picked out of the minds of their dupes, and presented as messages from dead friends.

As I am writing this, I have seated in my study a very intelligent Hindoo lady, and she corroborates what I have always held, that the feats so often ascribed to the occultism of the Hindoos, of seeing men throw ropes into the air, and then swarming up them; making tamarind trees grow at once before your eyes, and all those marvellous 'tricks' supposed to be done by the 'adepts,' so beloved of Theosophists, are all worked by hypnotism, by processes she has never heard explained. Many of the bystanders are hypnotized, and made, by adroit suggestion, to believe they see things which are only subjective and not objective; the creation of their own thought, and not actual existences.

If, then, the human mind is capable of these impressions, it is not stating an impossible suggestion that the healing of maladies due to nerval derangement is perfectly possible by the reading of Mrs. Eddy's mesmerizing book, or even by the mental suggestion of an absent healer, who usually puts her patient en rapport with herself by arranging the hour of the treatment. This hypnotic restraint of the 'active' mind sets free the 'subjective' mind to work, with its strange power, the 'suggestion' impressed upon it.

CHAPTER V.

THE DOCTRINE OF "CHRISTIAN SCIENCE."

A COUNTERFEIT dollar bill frequently passes current, and as long as its falseness is undetected it will purchase exactly as much as its legitimate represe:.tative. The possessor of the bill is quite satisfied with it. He rejoices in its possession, and until an expert discovers the fraud, and he suddenly becomes aware that his money has vanished, and he only possesses a piece of very dirty paper, he builds his hopes upon it. He may be depending upon it to defray a pressing liability. Imagine his revulsion of feeling when, at the moment he most needs it, it proves worthless, and leaves him unable to pay his lawful debt, a hopeless bankrupt!

A no more momentous question can any one consider, than, upon what his hopes for eternity are built. Has he any certain assurance that when he closes his eyes on this world, he will be with Jesus Christ and his servants in Paradise, in the next world?

In three chapters in S. Matthew's Gospel we have preserved for us "The Sermon on the Mount." It is the authoritative declaration by our Lord, wherein his teaching differed from that inculcated by the clergy of the day. A great many things they taught with which He agreed; these He does not mention;

there is nothing here about public worship, although it was his wont to attend, and probably regularly attend, the Synagogue service. "Wist ye not," said He to his anxious mother, "that I must be in my Father's house?" There is nothing here about offering sacrifices and the ritual of ceremonial worship. And yet He came not to destroy, but to fulfill the Law. Those who flatter themselves that their "forsaking the assembling of themselves together" finds sanction from the Sermon on the Mount are grievously mistaken. This proclamation, together with the undisputed requirements of the Law, common to the teaching of our Lord and the Scribes, is an authoritative statement of the religion revealed in the Word of God. This is the declaration by Him, who best knew, how the men of the earth may enter the Kingdom of God.

At the end of his sermon he gathered the principles he had been announcing and illustrating into a practical application; and if we were not so familiar with the words, they would take away our breath every time we read them. He says: "Not everyone that saith unto me, Lord, Lord, shall enter into the Kingdom of Heaven, but he that doeth the will of my Father, which is in heaven."

There are people who say that Jesus of Nazareth never laid claim to Divinity; they surely never read this passage. With what awful wonder must some of those who heard Him that day have listened, as that quiet-looking countryman, without any voluble asseveration, declared that He was the Judge of all the earth!

"Many will say to Me in that day, Lord, Lord,

have we not prophesied in thy name? and in thy name have cast out devils? and in thy name have done many wonderful works?

Then will I profess unto them, I never knew you; depart from Me, ye that work iniquity."

There is little doubt that the presence of the last word, "iniquity," has hitherto deprived this passage of its vital moment. If "preaching in Christ's name" and "casting out devils" and "doing many wonderful works" be counted "iniquity," then the passage cannot be worthy of serious attention, and so it is put out of mind, as that with which we have no practical concern. But "iniquity" is not the literal rendering of the word, it really means "without law;" that what they advanced as reasons for being admitted into the habitations of the just were not accepted because they were not done lawfully, they had not the imprimatur of the right motive. This rendered them counterfeit, and therefore worthless. So that, to preach the Gospel of Jesus Christ; to live to withstand and undo the "works of the devil," which bring on mankind sorrow and sickness; to live so unselfishly as to spend and be spent for others; to be an energetic, successful, and liberal philanthropist; to do what men call "good works," is of no avail, unless all is done from a right motive.

The whole question turns on our personal knowledge of Jesus Christ. If we can say with S. Paul, "I know Him whom I have believed," then and then only shall we work with the right motive, the love of personal service to a personal Master; without this, all else is sounding brass and a tinkling cymbal—and whatever may have been our experiences here, if we

THE DOCTRINE OF "CHRISTIAN SCIENCE." 59

know not the Lord, we shall learn our eternal doom from the other side of the closed door: "I never knew you, depart all ye that work unlawfully"—Matt. vii., 23.

What we have to examine is, first, the works professed to be done by "Christian Scientists;" and then whether the motives which prompted them are those found described and illustrated in the Bible.

It is not with the smart pen of a controversialist that I approach this difficult subject, but I would rather ask my reader to believe I am concerned to state in the best form the "Christian Science" position, and with all loving anxiety to indicate where the "unlawfulness" is to be found; the "unlawfulness" which proves the counterfeit, and jeopardizes the salvation of many truth-seeking souls.

For the sake of perspicuity, as well as brevity, I shall confine my examination to the text book of the cult, "Science and Health, with Key to the Scriptures," by Mary Baker G. Eddy, Boston, edition 74. I restrict myself to this work, for all practical purposes the statement of the "Science" is here sufficient, and as I suppose from the following passage, which it would be easy to support by a hundred others, this book is the admitted and undisputed text book of the Society. In the October, 1895, number of the "Christian Science Journal," published by "The Christian Science" Publishing Society, it is said:

> Surely the people of the coming centuries will vie with each other in doing homage to the Rev. Mary Baker Eddy, the greatest character since the advent of Jesus the Christ, and her book, "Science and Health, with Key to the Scriptures," will go down in history as a part of the sacred writings of the ages.

This book is fondly called "The Little Book," in allusion to that "little book" which the mighty angel in Revelations x., 8, had in his hand and gave to the Divine Apostle to eat. (Page 538.)

For a statement of the works alleged to have been done by "Christian Science" I quote from a tract issued by the Boston authority. It exhibits the seal of the Society, and its title is "Religious Eras;" this is the description, " of course in part anticipative," of the characteristics and results "of the religion known by the name of 'Christian Science:'"

Suppose we had a religion we were glad to talk about whenever and wherever we met; that should become to us an all-absorbing theme; that should so interest us that, when we met together for purposes of religious worship, we should be so full of brotherly love and good-fellowship, so full of the fraternal feeling growing out of our religious thought and association, that we should feel loath to separate at the conclusion of the services, and repair to our homes. Suppose that, as the result of our religion, we should live for each other in a larger sense than we ever before dreamed of; that all social follies and frivolities should become so distasteful that, as a mere matter of choice, we should no longer care to participate in them.

Suppose that this religion should enlarge our mental scope and elevate our taste to one for a higher and better class of literature; that it should bring us a single book which, with the Bible, should become so useful and helpful to us in our every-day life, that we should never tire of reading. Suppose that, as the result of reading this book and the Scriptures in the new light which it should give us, our natures should become so transformed that we should lose all taste for gossip, all love for idleness, all desire for unnecessary display; should lose so much of self, that the keen desire to live only for money-getting should pass away, until we could and would honestly say with Agassiz: " I have no time to make money."

Suppose the reading of the little book to which I have

referred, should open our eyes to the fact that in all our past life we have been living almost wholly for self; that, so selfish had we been, we had brought misery not only upon ourselves but upon those coming in contact with us in our daily lives. Suppose it should open our eyes to the fact that we had been all our lives envying our neighbor, coveting his possessions, and wishing we could have as many good things, and enjoy life as well as he. Suppose it should open our eyes to the fact that we had been all our lives slaves to foolish and hurtful passions and appetites; that in all our past lives we had been the victims of foolish fear—fear of this thing and fear of that, fear of sickness and death, fear of lightning and tempest, fear for our own safety and that of our friends, and especially of our children. Suppose, as the result of understanding this little book, we should awaken to the fact that our whole previous life had been one prolonged nightmare of foolish and unnecessary fear; that all the agony we had suffered in consequence was the result of our ignorance of what true life and true religion are.

Suppose the little book should cause us to realize that much, indeed nearly all, of the misery and unhappiness we had suffered was the result of our own depraved will; that a part, and very considerable part, of this depraved will was the result of a foolish human pride—a pride as profitless as silly. Suppose it should open our eyes to the fact that almost all the time, often quite unconsciously to ourselves, as the result of this depraved will, we had been in the habit of practicing deceit; not only upon others, in ways that seemed harmless to them, as well as in ways we knew might or would injure, but, in our blindness, upon ourselves—flattering ourselves that we were having great success therein. Suppose that the little book startled us with the discovery that we had actually been the victims of the most intense hatred—hatred of our neighbor, hatred of ourselves—our own worst enemies; that it opened our eyes to the fact that we had been so full of revenge, that we had almost let the thought of murder get possession of us; that we actually would have felt relieved for the moment if some dire calamity had befallen the object of our hatred.

Suppose we should have this experience; and then suppose

the little book should, after having laid bare our faults and shortcomings, so work upon us that these things would become so hideous and distasteful that we should of our own preference set about overcoming them; and further, that the more we strove in that direction the happier we should be, because our striving now actually brought about results plainly perceptible to ourselves and to our friends, so that even those who did not believe in our religion could but notice and comment upon our improved appearance and changed character. Suppose that the understanding of this little book so opened our eyes to the truth, beauty, and grandeur of the Bible, that, whereas it was before an obscure and almost meaningless fable, it now became a great light fresh from the hand of God, illuminating our heretofore dull and weary pathway; that, in consequence, we breathed a new atmosphere, saw with new eyes, heard with new ears, walked with new limbs, talked with a new tongue, thought new thoughts with a mind that had taken on a new vesture.

Suppose that, as the result of our understanding the little book, we were brought into consciousness of a relationship with God, of which we had never before been able to conceive; that we realized a nearness to and a companionship with Him, that seemed utterly beyond our grasp in the old conditions; until we could, from our own experience, declare Him to be, in truth and in fact, Omniscience, Omnipotence and Omnipresence—an ever-present, practical Help in time of actual need. And, in addition to all this, suppose that we should, as the result of reading and understanding the little book, prove able not only to heal ourselves of sickness, and afterward keep ourselves free from attacks of sickness, but could heal our friends, and aid them in keeping themselves free from disease. Suppose, as the result of this kind of a religion, we were able to destroy in people the appetite for intoxicating drink, for tobacco, for gambling, for debauchery of every kind—in short, for all kinds of foolish and hurtful expenditure of time and money.

Suppose that these things could be accomplished presently; and that, beyond all this, we could see such mighty possibilities for the uplifting and regeneration of the human race right here on this plane of existence as poverty of language renders impossible of expression, and finite sense impossible of conception. Suppose this, I say (and there are many other suppositions in which we might properly indulge, but time forbids), and would not all unite in claiming this to be a true religion, the religion that the world needs; a religion, indeed, "of the people, for the people, and by the people;" a fulfilling of prophecy, and, in fact, the religion of Jesus Christ?

This is, indeed, an entrancing and magnificent description of the "new earth," and if only there was anything of a hope "full of immortality," anything about a "new heaven," we, too, should feel it "our grand privilege and blessed work to spread this precious new Gospel." But it is exactly here, where most we need, that we have no teaching, no promise. "The little book" is mentioned ten times, and twice only, as if apologetically thrown in, is "with the Scriptures." The Word of God, which alone has brought "life and immortality" to mankind, is altogether superseded by "the little book." Not a word is said of Him who bringeth in righteousness, except to assert that this "Christian Science" is the religion of Jesus Christ.

Let us now search its text book, to learn the distinguishing marks of this Gospel, and see whether it be the Gospel of Christ, which S. Paul preached; or is it "another gospel," and is it against the author of "the little book" and others like her that the great Apostle delivers himself so emphatically: "Though we, or an angel from heaven, preach any other Gospel unto you than that we have preached unto you, let him be accursed"? Gal. i., 8.

CHAPTER VI.

MAN.

AS the object of this Gospel is the ameliorating of the condition of man, let us first try to learn what Mrs. Eddy would have us believe man is.

Words in philosophic writing must have fixed values. They are to the philosopher what numbers are to the mathematician; if they do not bear the same meaning in the same book, the work becomes as worthless as if, in a mathematical treatise, the symbols 3 and 5 and 7 were used indiscriminately. This is a great cause of indistinctness in Mrs. Eddy's writings; she not only uses words to convey other meanings than are commonly current, but continually the same word must have another meaning than that in which it was used on the previous page, or the sentence is inexplicable. As she uses "man" in two very different senses, it is very difficult to understand her theory. Page 291, she says:

> When man is spoken of as made in God's image, it is not the sinful and sickly mortal man who is referred to, but the ideal man, reflected as God's likeness.

We immediately suppose that "man," then, means unfallen man, Adam before he sinned; but not so, for she complains of some critic in this same paragraph that he *confounds man with Adam.* Then "man," in her use, refers to an ideal man. Page 491 :

> Man is the family name for all the sons and daughters of God.

Then, there are no sons and daughters of God in reality, but they exist as "ideals."

It is evident that these blessed beings do not belong to our life, for on page 198 she says:

> The science of Being reveals man as perfect, even as the Father is perfect, because the soul, or mind of man, is God, the Divine Principle of his Being, and the real man is governed by this soul, instead of sense; by the law of spirit, and not of matter.

It is quite clear from this that "man" here referred to, is not such as we are, for we all eat, and in this are governed by sense, and if we did not eat we should not be here.

Where, then, is this "man"? Is the ideal man inside the man we know? It would appear so. And it is the office of "Christian Science" to draw this divine being to the surface, and make him take the governance of our personality. Page 426:

> The great spiritual fact must be brought out that man *is*, not *shall be*, perfect and immortal. We must hold forever the consciousness of existence, and sooner or later, aided by "Christian Science," we must master sin, disease, and death.

This means to say that within a human being is a "man." This man is, indeed, the Deity Himself. Page 154:

> Mortals have a very feeble and imperfect idea of the spiritual man and the infinite range of his thoughts. To him belongs eternal life. Never born and never dying, it is an impossibility for Being, under the government of eternal science, to fall from its high estate.

Page 461:

Man is co-existent with God.

Page 459:

Man is incapable of sin, sickness, and death, inasmuch as he derives his essence from God, and possesses not a single original or underived power. Hence the real man cannot depart from holiness. Nor can God, by whom man was evolved, engender the capacity or freedom to sin. A mortal sinner is not God's man, for the offspring of God cannot be evil. Mortals are man's counterfeits. They are the children of the Wicked One, or the one evil, which declares that man begins as a material embryo.

Mortals, then, are evidently men and women as we see them. They are counterfeits of the real, divine man, who is somewhere enshrouded in the human being, and which it is the prerogative of "Christian Science" to bring into evidence. But how did the counterfeit come into existence? Mrs. Eddy tells us that it is the child of the Wicked One. It will not avail her to immediately obscure her statement by defining the Wicked One to be "the one evil," for "Wicked One" and "one evil" are by no stretch of imagination the same thing; the one is an Agent, who begat the "Mortal," and the other is a quality; and a quality can do nothing. But we are not left to surmise what she means, for we are plainly told on page 460 that

Mortals are not fallen children of God. They never had a perfect state of Being, which may be subsequently regained. They were, from the beginning of mortal history, conceived in sin and brought forth in iniquity.

That is, by the Wicked One.

Mortals are material falsities. In the words of Paul, they are "without hope and without God in the world." They are errors made up of sin, sickness, and death, which must disappear to give place to the facts which belong to immortal man.

Page 505:
Could spirit evolve its opposite, matter, and give ability to sin and suffering? . . . . . Does Mind, God, enter matter, to become there a mortal sinner, animated by the breath of God? . . . . . Man represents God; mankind represents the Adamic race, and is a human, not a Divine creation.

What Mrs. Eddy wants to prove is quite clear. Her idea is that man is the creation of God, and as such a part of Himself, and therefore in reality possessing all that He is; perfect wholeness, goodness, etc. She even, compelled by her theory, asserts that he is "co-existent with God," that he is "never born," and is "never dying," and in spite of her assertion on page 464, that "Man is not God," this means that he is "a partaker of the Divine nature," and is God!

But the experience of life exhibits man to be a very different being. Uncivilized human nature is the very antipodes of "goodness;" savages are very devils; and all men are born and all men die. Therefore, to accommodate her theory to the facts of human life, she is compelled to assume the visible man, who is too evidently wicked and feeble and dying, to be not of "Divine creation." In the quotations we have cited she ascribes his origin to two sources, the "Wicked One" and "human creation." And as her object is to deal and deal only with the divine man, there is nothing left for her but to declare that man, as we know him, is a phantom, an illusion, and not real. She found support for this view in the fact that this "mortal man," who must have a creator, for it is out of the question for nothing to make something, cannot be brought into existence by God, "good," "all-good." Therefore his existence is due to one of the only two other agents she appears to have heard of, "The Wicked One" and "man himself." But, as geology assures us that this planet once was without life, there was a time when there was not such a being as "mortal man;" hence there is nothing for it but to allow that the origin of this "material falsity," this "counterfeit of man," is the work of "The Wicked One," and this marvellous deception is only what is to be expected, seeing that "he is the father of lies." The "mortal man," that is, man as we see him, is, then, a very wonderful construction of deception; he is a being who transacts his business in the world, and apparently does as he likes. There is in him an intelligence which regulates his life, but this very intelligence is itself marvellously adapted to carry out the grand deception—an assumption which is essential to the working of the theory. This intelligence is called "mortal mind." We are told on page 40 that this "mortal mind" is "the autocrat of the body." It "governs every organ of the mortal body;" indeed, so intimately are the two connected that (page 70) "mortal mind and body are one." This "mortal mind" builds its own body, which "from first to last is only a sensuous belief," and upon which (page 401) it is constantly producing the results of false belief; "this it accomplishes through the five physical senses," which (page 170) "are simply beliefs of mortal mind."

That is, that whatever appears to affect us which would disturb our peace or our comfort is nothing but the illusion of "mortal mind" reaching us through senses which it has purposely devised for this shameful deception, and all we have to do is to refuse to be deceived; to roundly assert that we are under delusion, that there is no such thing as sin, sickness, and death, and in time the real man within us will shake off the nightmare that has seized us, and we shall awake into the light and liberty of the Kingdom of God, our true Father. It is the mission of "Christian Science" to work out for us this salvation. It is needless to say that this theory has no support from any other source; that the common sense of mankind derides it, and the continual death and burial of "Christian Scientists" declare it without foundation.

But it is time to compare the "Scientists'" theory with the statements of their "text-book," the Word of God, corroborated as they are by the experiences of humanity. The Wisdom of Solomon ii., 23, 24, states concisely what the rest of the Bible reveals: "God created man to be immortal, and made him to be an image of his own eternity. Nevertheless, through the envy of the devil came death into the world; and they that do hold of his side do find it."

It is unnecessary to multiply texts. S. Paul declares, what is held by all spiritually enlightened men, that "By one man sin entered into the world, and death by sin," Rom. v., 12. The admission of sin, which was the act of the unfettered will of our first parents, vitiated our nature, and made man, not what the "Scientists" declare him to be, the offspring of God, with his nature and prerogatives, but of a nature similar to his tempter. Jesus Christ stated it concisely, "Ye are of your father, the devil." Man fell from the condition which he was first created to maintain, and he became wholly sinful. Any sin completely destroys holiness. He once was pronounced by his Maker to be "very good," but after his disobedience that same Maker declared that "every imagination of the thoughts of his heart was only evil continually," Gen. vi., 5.

Mrs. Eddy is constantly declaring that as God is omnipotent He cannot be withstood of evil; that, in truth, there cannot be any evil to withstand Him; and yet she asks us to believe that "Man," himself a very part of God, is enveloped by a phantom form, the cunning device of the Wicked One, and in this "material falsity" is caused to reside all those delusions and "mortal beliefs" which make the passage of this life little else than a 'Vale of Tears.' How can this be credited? Surely the Divine Being could not be thus restrained, and especially by that which, at least He must know, has no reality.

Not a few of Mrs. Eddy's followers have felt the impossibility of this assumption, and therefore "there was a division among them," which Scriptural assertion they may possibly construe to give warrant for the establishment of "Centres of Divine Healing." The one in Denver, which was dedicated by the Western prophetess of the "Science," Mrs. Cramer, of San Francisco, is out of harmony with the "Church of Christ (Scientist)." She has put forth a book, "Lessons in Science and Healing," and has proved herself such an adept at mystic writing that she and her husband issue the most credited magazine of the cult, "Harmony."

On page 20 of this we read·

"There is one God and Father of all, Who is above all,

and through all, and in you all."—Eph. iv., 6. The limitless goodness is uncreate Being. This excludes the possibility of there being another life, substance or power. There are no powers that are not good, "for the powers that be are ordained of God."

A belief in two powers, one Good and the other Evil, one warring against the other, and a belief that matter is life, and has powers and laws that are opposed to infinite spirit, is the division which causes all desolation. The belief that we have a lower and higher nature, one warring with the other, or that we have a lower self and a higher self, each striving to rule, is a house divided against itself. This belief has brought desolation, division and delusion upon humanity . . . . . Ignorance, or the lack of understanding in expression, is the source of the erroneous race belief in two powers, for this belief is judgment rendered on authority of what the senses reveal—intellectual reasoning. And just the opposite of the testimony of the senses is Divine Truth.

Mrs. Cramer is more cautious than Mrs. Eddy. She ventures on no hypothesis how it comes to pass that we have been invested with senses for the express purpose of deceiving us; she is content to make the assertion, and thereafter keep clear of an obscure and disagreeable subject.

But this is the common belief of all "Scientists," that the testimony of the senses is contrary to the fact of divine wholeness, which must be the condition of the real man; that it is only necessary to shake off this delusion, and the true state of absolute perfection will be enjoyed. It is not worth while to point to the anatomy of the organs of sense, and indicate the similarity of their contrivances to the corresponding organs in animals; and to point to the patent fact that they serve us in the same manner as they serve the animals, who have no divine nature to shroud in delusion. But, inasmuch as even "Scientists" admit that Jesus Christ is the Truth; indeed, Mrs. Eddy declares that "the coming of Christ was the appearance of Truth," He was "the highest human concept of a perfect man . . . the divine idea of God, outside of the flesh;" then surely He must have been aware of the illusion practiced by the senses; yet He drops no hint of their faithlessness. Nay, he always appeals to their evidence in support of his claims: "Hearken unto Me," "Handle Me and see," "Lift up your eyes and behold."

The Lord Jesus cannot be cited as a favorable witness in support of the "Scientists'" theory.

It would be impossible for this compound man to remain under closest inspection all these centuries, and yet not exhibit some sign of the strange duality. Now, when such an intensely interesting and bold biological theory is broached, its only chance of serious examination by the intelligent world would be to support it by an array of accurate observations.

The prodigious accumulation of accurate observation is a large part of the claim for respect which Mr. Darwin makes of his fellow-man. What claim has Mrs. Eddy upon our serious attention? She not only cites no proofs of any kind, but she reveals to us her total incapacity for observation. It would be, indeed, inexplicable that people incapable of thinking, and uneducated, should give any heed to her statements, but that intelligent crowds, who have had the benefit of the public school education, should listen to "readers," properly accredited and salaried, for the very purpose of reading "the little book," is as strange a vagary of human nature as the history of it has ever produced. To judge of the calibre of Mrs. Eddy's mind, and her real capability for observation, read this astonishing paragraph on page 537:

> It is related that a father, anxious to try this experiment, plunged his infant babe, only a few hours old, into water for several minutes, and repeated this operation daily, until the child could remain under water twenty minutes, moving and playing without harm, like a fish. Parents should remember this, and so learn to develop their children properly on dry land!

Let any one hold their breath even for *one* minute, and they can estimate the value of the rest of Mrs. Eddy's assertions.

All the children of Adam were born outside Paradise. We are particularly told that when in this condition "Adam begat a son after his own likeness and in his own image," Gen. v., 3. The descending course of human life has shown no signs of its returning to its pristine purity. David said exactly what the history tells us of the near descendants of Adam: "Behold, I was shapen in iniquity, and in sin did my mother conceive me," Psalm li., 5. And another thousand years of human experience have shown no improvement whatever. S. Paul stated his observation, "All have sinned and come short of the glory of God," Rom. iii., 23; which is practically the same language as David used: "They are all gone aside; they are altogether become filthy; there is none that doeth good; no, not one," Psalm xiv., 3.

If any one thinks that the race shows to-day any tendency to betterment, let him gain an accurate knowledge of the lives, say, of the Chinese, a people of an ancient civilization, and with a system of education such as the world has never seen, by which every post of Government, from the lowest official to the Taoti of a Province, can only be had by public examination. S. Paul's description of the heathen world, as he knew it, is the description of the heathen world to-day, where it has not been influenced by an atmosphere of public opinion cleared by the morals of Christianity. Read the latter half of the first chapter of his Epistle to the Romans, weigh the actual meaning of each sentence, and it is a fearful indictment — " they have altogether become filthy "!

It was to this world, "lying in wickedness," that God came as a Saviour. And what is the plan of his salvation? Not the development of the Divine germ, smothered and overborne by an accumulation of "fleshly lust;" not the liberation of "the true man" from the grasp of his false double; not the enlightening of "the spiritual consciousness" of the real man, by the revelations vouchsafed to Mrs. Eddy, that he may fling off the trammels of " mortal mind," and rise from the charnel house of "sin, sickness and death," to walk in the liberty wherewith " Christian Science " hath made him free. To preach this were " another gospel." The gospel of the grace of God is the narration of the Incarnation, the death and the resurrection of the second Person of the Blessed Trinity, the Son of God. It is the assertion of the mode of production of a new kind of vitality. It is the statement of the process, as seen from a human point of view, of the modification of the divine life so that it could express itself through a body of this flesh. It is the solution of the problem how to make the material and immaterial worlds sentient of each other.

The Lord Jesus Christ took down the middle wall of partition, and in Him the two worlds joined. He was "the Son of Man" who is in heaven. Just as He could say to Philip, "He that hath seen Me hath seen the Father," so he could say to the Intelligences of the Unseen World, "He that hath seen Me hath seen humanity." This is not a supposition, but it is the central truth of the Bible, which is called "the Book of this life." The last of the inspired writers states the purport of the whole compilation: "This is the record, that God hath given us eternal life, and this life is in His Son. He that hath the Son hath life, and he that hath not the Son of God hath not life."

Now, it would be a thankless boon to bestow upon us as "a gift" that which we already possessed. If we had in us "eternal life," why cause the inexpressible sacrifice of the Son of God to provide it for us? Nothing is clearer in the Word of God, that "we have no life in us;" that we are "dead in trespasses and sins;" our English preposition "in" is a very feeble representative of its Greek parent; in its original is included the agency by which the condition was acquired; it is "the trespasses and sins" which keep us "dead." In this state "life" is presented to us; that will, which our first parents used to do the deed of disobedience, has still the same liberty, and can accept this gift of eternal life if it so wills. Therefore, our Lord stood in the midst of the human procession and cried: "Ye will not to come unto Me, that ye might have life," John v., 40. As might be expected, when this life was accepted by anyone, then the only word we have to express the inheritance of life comes to be used — he is said to be "born from above," John iii., 3. Or, to use S. Paul's words, "And you, who were dead, hath He quickened," Ephes. ii., 1. It is a question of the impartation of life, a new vitality. S. Paul, describing one who has received it, declares him to be "a new creation," a totally new being, vitalized with another kind of life. The Apostle asserts: "The life I now live in the flesh, I live by the faith of the Son of God; and when Christ, who is my life, shall appear, then shall I also appear with Him in glory," Gal. ii., 20.

This life carries with it the marks of any other vitality. It has a character of its own, from which it never deviates. This character was most thoroughly displayed in Jesus of Nazareth. But the instant it finds lodgment in any heart, it there and then begins to produce a character more and more approaching His, as the life more and more gains command of the man. This is a very singular biological fact, and one which has not received the attention it deserves. It matters not who may be the subject of its influence, learned or unlearned, young or old, civilized or savage, the Esquimo of the Arctic zone or the negro of the tropics; at once is exhibited, despite the varied conditions of race, temperament, tradition or environment, the self-same character, whose elements are "love, joy, peace, long-suffering, gentleness, goodness, faith, disinterestedness, temperance." This is so real and so certain, that S. Paul points to that other mark of true life, the determination to reproduce its original, and accounts for the invariable exhibition of these traits of character by saying that "Christ is formed in us." This is the declaration of "the text book" of the "Christian Scientists," and it is as far from what they profess to have found in it as well-nigh can be imagined. Any one of the quotations already cited is quite sufficient to discredit their impossible theory. But if any one has any lingering doubt, let him consider the meaning of the words of S. John i., 11, etc. The Divine Apostle says that his Master was that "life" which was the "light" of men; that "He came to His own, and His own received Him not; but as many as received Him, to them gave He authority to be called sons of God, even to them that believe in His name;" that is, that when He, the life, found entrance to an open heart, that being, by virtue of the life, became united in living union with the origin of that life, and therefore had the right, the authority, to be classed as a son of God. And this marvellous condition was not acquired by any possible human effort; it was not a development of that which was already in human nature; it could not be come by, by any process of training in "science," or any other mode of initiation; but it was wholly a gracious gift of God. "Which were born not of blood;" we did not inherit this Christ-life from our parents; "nor of the will of flesh;" this is by no means a repetition of what has just been stated; but "of flesh," without the article, was the Jewish mode of referring to circumcision, and all the ceremonial which followed upon it. The Apostle tells us that this "Divine seed" is not got by any ceremonial, or sacrament, or church privilege; "nor of the will of man;" no human effort or device will cause a soul thus to be born into the family of God; there is one, and only one way; it is the soul itself opening to receive Jesus Christ, it is thus "of God." "Behold, I stand at the door and knock, and if any man open the door, we will come in to him and sup with him."

This is the natural history of redeemed man as given in the Bible, and it bears no likeness whatever to that taught by "Scientists."

"I speak to wise men, judge ye what I say."

CHAPTER VII.

THE HOLY GHOST.

WE must bear in mind that "Christian Science" and its relatives profess not only to take the Bible for their text book, but that its deep and spiritual meaning is revealed to them in fuller measure than to those who study it in the usual way.

Everyone who is led by the Spirit of God naturally has a delight in seeking the Mind of God as revealed in His Word. The experiences of Bible students is uniform, that "spiritual things are spiritually revealed;" that it is not to mere human intelligence and persistent study that the Bible yields up its precious treasures, but it is by the illumination of the Spirit that the sacred page becomes perspicuous, and what to the ordinary reader is an intellectual reception, to the true child of God becomes "a living word;" and at once acknowledgment is made that "The entrance of Thy Word giveth light." Of this prominent peculiarity of the true Christian the "Christian Scientist" is provided with a close counterfeit. This it is which most deceives the religiously inclined, the mere formal Christian, as it is shown that the study of the Bible is the ardent practice of "Scientists." To the unwary this appears a sure sign that "the thing is of God." But it is a counterfeit sign.

The Baconian figment of the authorship of Shakespeare lately had a transient passage over the literary sky. Had anyone seen Mr. Ignatius Donnelly and his co-believers diligently conning their Shakespeares, it would have been a fair deduction that they were devoted students of the great poet. But they were not. What attracted them was only to search for apparent proofs of the novel theory which they had adopted. So it is with "Scientists"; they do not study the Bible humbly and reverently to learn, "What will the Lord say to me?" but to find support for the vagaries of their "Science of Being," and to twist the English translation of a Greek book to fit the crannies and turns of their desultory, tortuous theory.

If they declare the Bible to be their "text book," and if they are ever ready to cite from its pages what they think is in their favor, they cannot object to honestly measuring their tenets by its express statements. There is scarcely any more vital revelation to us, living in this Dispensation, than the position occupied by the Holy Ghost in the present governance of the Church. When Jesus was glorified, the Holy Spirit, "the other advocate," descended to undertake the personal direction of the Church. So persistently is He referred to in the Acts of the Apostles, that that book might well be called "The Acts of the Holy Ghost." He came with irresistible power on the day of Pentecost, and remained on earth. The Apostles continued in Jerusalem, a college, for twenty years, bearing witness, in the only place on earth where their witness could be refuted, to the Resurrection. S. Peter well knew the immense necessity of this institution. He said to the Sanhedrim: "And we are his witnesses of these things; and so also is the Holy Ghost," Acts v., 32. When they sat in council it is almost as if the Kingdom of God were at length "set up" on earth, and the royal throne in the council chamber possessed in actual sight the August Majesty. The very first edict they issued, which was to lay to rest the burning question of the time, whether the Gentile converts should first become Jews before they could be admitted into the Church of Christ, begins: "It seemed good to the Holy Ghost and to us," Acts xv., 28.. They do not appear to deem any preface or explanation necessary; but, as if it were natural and well understood, they count the Holy Ghost as one of their number.

Throughout the whole book He is ever present in distinct personality. It was to the Holy Ghost Ananias and Sapphira lied; it was the Holy Ghost who spoke by the Apostles; it was the Holy Ghost the persecutors of Stephen resisted; it was that the men on whom Simon Magus should lay his hands might receive the Holy Ghost that he offered Peter money; it was the Holy Ghost who sent Philip to join himself to the Ethiopian Eunuch; it was the Holy Ghost who "caught away Philip" after his mission was fulfilled; it was the Holy Ghost who sent Peter to the Roman, Cornelius; it was the Holy Ghost who said, "Separate me Barnabas and Saul for the work whereunto I have called them;" it was the Holy Ghost who forbade them to preach the Word in Asia; it was the Holy Ghost who suffered them not to go into Bithynia; it was the Holy Ghost who, S. Paul declared to the Ephesian Elders, had made them overseers of the flock; and the whole narrative is full of the receiving of the gifts of the Holy Ghost.

That constant students of the Bible should fail to note the fact that the Holy Ghost is the Divine operator in that age, of which the Acts of the Apostles is the first historical page, and in which we are at present living, seems incredible. And when we learn that, as at the first creation, He it was who imparted life to this lifeless planet, so He presides over the birth of the new man, and the second creation is due to his life-giving energy; when we know that the whole initiative of salvation rests with Him, and that our eternal safety wholly depends upon the possession or the non-possession of the Holy Ghost, then it is strangely ominous that "Scientists" discard His personality and reduce His mighty agency to the intangibility of a "development of eternal life, Truth and Love," page 567.

This is so serious a charge that it becomes us to examine carefully what this "Science" does hold concerning the Holy Ghost.

In the Bible, Holy Ghost and Spirit are synonymous terms, but not so in "Divine Science." "Spirit" is defined, page 573, as:

Divine substance; mind; principle; all that is good; God; that only which is perfect, infinite, everlasting; omnipresent and omnipotent.

On page 230 we are told "Soul and Spirit are one." Whatever, therefore, may be meant by "Spirit," and it is not easy to say what Mrs. Eddy does mean, she certainly does not intend us to understand that when the word Spirit is used, the Holy Ghost of the Bible is meant.

Holy Ghost she defines on page 567 to be "Divine Science; the developments of eternal life, Truth and Love."

In recounting the salient features of our Lord's life in the light of "Divine Science," on page 351, she thus proceeds:

His students then received the Holy Ghost. By this is meant, that by all they had witnessed and suffered they were roused to an enlarged understanding of Divine Science. .... They no longer measured man by material sense. After gaining a true idea of their glorified Master they became better healers, leaning no longer on a leader, but on the Divine principle of their work. The influx of light was sudden. It was sometimes in overwhelming power, as on the day of Pentecost.

Page 348:

Hitherto they only believed; now they understood. This understanding is what is meant by the descent of the Holy Ghost, that influx of Divine Science which so illuminated the Pentecostal days, and is now repeating its ancient history.

On page 255 is given the platform of "Christian Science." Article X. is:

The Holy Ghost, or Spirit, reveals this triune Principle, and is expressed in Divine Science, which is the Comforter, leading into all truth, and revealing the Divine principle of the universe— universal and perpetual harmony.

It might be thought from the first of these quotations that Mrs. Eddy uses "Divine Science" as another appellation of the Holy Ghost, but we are precluded from accepting this by the statement on page 17 that

the re-discovery of this Divine Science of mind-healing, through a spiritual sense of the Scriptures and through the teachings of the Comforter, as promised by the Master, is one of the two parts of the revelation vouchsafed to Mrs. Eddy:

> When standing within the shadow of the Death Valley, I learned these truths in Divine Science.

If some of these expressions seem to recognize the personality of the Holy Ghost, this cannot be of deliberate purpose, and must be ascribed to a lapsus calami, in the presence of such repeated expressions as "the facts of Divine Science," "the mirror, Divine Science," "the Alpha and Omega of Divine Science."

There are only two other references, if the index be complete, to the Holy Ghost. In one, page 364, "the chambers of disease" appear to be called "The temple of the Holy Ghost," and the other is (page 334):

> The Holy Ghost, or Divine Spirit, overshadowed the pure sense of the Virgin-Mother with the full recognition that Being is Spirit.

What would be the Acts of the Apostles and the Epistles, if from them were eliminated all mention of the Holy Ghost? But "Science and Health, with Key to the Scriptures," would be very much benefited if the seven indistinct and uncertain allusions to Him were left out.

The conclusion is inevitably forced upon us, that this system of "Christian Science" has no place for the work of the Holy Ghost; and as He alone is the "Lord and Life-Giver," as without Him there can be no life unto God, no birth into the Kingdom of Christ, no process of sanctification, and no final holiness, "without which no man shall see the Lord," the relation between "Christian Science" and Christianity seems but nominal.

CHAPTER VIII

SPIRIT.

IF Mrs. Eddy had written with even any attempt at exactness, her book and her 'science' would never have had the success they have. A perusal of the pages of this remarkable book will reveal to the person of ordinary intelligence that that quality of the mind which is called 'thought' is here so persistently defied, that at length it retires from endeavoring to understand what the authoress means, and in that bewilderment which then ensues, the mind surrenders itself to that very condition which is essential for the operation of 'suggestion' to work upon the disordered body.

I found that Mrs. Eddy's book was the best mode of inducing the mesmeric sleep I had ever experienced. The repetition of senseless sentences, with constantly changing signification of words, whose new meanings had to be gleaned from the context; this long string of synonyms: Principle; Mind; Soul; Spirit; Life; Truth; Love; Substance; Intelligence; are all synonyms for God, and their interchange in sentences produced a strange maze, which made the mind dazed, and it took on the mesmeric condition. When in this state, the 'subjective' mind was liberated to follow 'suggestion.' Of course this process will only be effective with certain people. Those who decline to read unless they understand, declare the book to be rubbish, and throw it aside; but those who are not particular about fathoming what they read, accept what Mrs. Eddy has written, yield themselves to the misty labyrinth of her sentences, become mentally dizzy, though they do not recognize it—mesmerized, in fact. It is a condition not unallied to intoxication, and is as enthralling and attractive.

Not long ago I heard that a young professional man of great promise, who was, and indeed is, afflicted with such nervousness that he is unable to control his muscular movements, was attending the "Church of Christ" (Scientist). I asked him if he had accepted the theories there propounded. He replied, smiling, "Well, no; but you know how nervous I am, and I find going there mesmerizes me, and I sit quiet."

In thus writing, I am not making unwarrantable aspersions on Mrs. Eddy's indiscriminate use of words, and the playfulness with which she treats their etymology. I quote from page 233, a plank from her 'platform:'

The word Adam is from the Hebrew Adamah, signifying the *red color of the ground, dust, nothingness.* Divide the name Adam into two syllables and it reads *a dam*, or obstruction. This suggests the thought of something fluid, of mortal mind in solution, of the darkness which seemed to appear when "darkness was upon the face of the deep," and matter stood as opposed to spirit, as that which is accursed.

Despite the fact that lucidity would render inoperative the whole system, there must be some people among the 200,000 'Scientists' who believe that Mrs.

Eddy's terms are to be seriously taken, and that definite meanings are to be ascribed to her phrases.

We now reach the keynote of the "Science," Spirit. It will be well to remind ourselves that there are certain ideas which the human mind is not constructed to entertain. Infinity, for instance. No number can be conceived to which it is not possible to add a unit; no space can be thought of to which an extension cannot be imagined. Spirit, too, lies beyond the grasp of the human mind. We are so familiar with the word, that we have come to believe we have a conception of Spirit; but let the attempt be made to form a mental picture of Spirit, and it will be found impossible. We receive all our ideas from sensation and reflection; but as we have no sensation of Spirit, the mind is not supplied with the elements from which to construct its idea.

The body has been under our closest scrutiny for these six thousand years, and as yet scientific observation has not been able to note any single fact about "life," the spiritual power which drives the marvellous mechanism. The complete seclusion in which this spiritual force secretes itself is the more remarkable when we consider its wonderful strength; the human heart is worked by it with a force which could lift 25 foot-tons in twenty-four hours. Few people comprehend the terrific energy of this unseen occupier of the human frame. When we consider this, and remember that the governor of this seething corporation has never been brought forth to view, although he has been unweariedly sought for, it ought to make us cautious in our use of the word Spirit.

Matter would seem to be the bête noire of the

'scientists.' Mrs. Eddy views matter as not only the opposite of Spirit, but its determined antagonist. She is unable to see how the Creator, himself Spirit, can ever have brought into existence so unspiritual a thing as matter. But what is impossible to Mrs. Eddy and her following may not be so difficult to minds otherwise educated. On page 174 she writes:

> Is Spirit the source or creator of matter? Science reveals nothing in Spirit out of which to create matter.
> Science destroys matter. Spirit is the only substance and consciousness recognized by Science.
> The senses oppose this, but there are no material senses, for matter has no sensation. To Science there is no matter, even as to truth there is no error, and to good no evil.
> It is a false supposition, the notion that there is real *substance-matter*, the opposite of Spirit. Spirit is God, and God is all; hence He can have no opposite.

This last sentence contains the central falsity upon which pivots the whole theory of "Christian Science:" "Spirit is God, and God is all; therefore all is Spirit." "Spirit is God" may be true, if, to adopt the language of theological science, the substance of the Deity is Spirit. Our Lord said to the woman at the well, in order to impress upon her that materialism was not the great question, for all her religion was a matter of facts and forms, that "God is Spirit," not *a* Spirit. But to say that whatever being is composed of spirit is God, is not true; for there are evil intelligences who are of spirit, and vast orders of life which people the unseen world. So that what we ought to say is, Some Spirit is God.

Then, again, to say "*God is all*," is not true. Our Lord, only to refer to one of his assertions, said to those who resisted Him, "Ye are of your father, the devil;" and even if the "Scientists" will not allow the existence of the devil, there are many men who have not a spark of goodness in them. "God is not in all their thoughts." These inhabit that land of Nod, where Cain and his following live in forgetfulness of God, and are "without God" in their world. So God is not all.

The "Scientists" seem to forget that the very necessity of Love is, that it shall have some being on whom to rest its affections. That God, being Love, was compelled to people the universe with personalities, whom He might love. Such personalities must have freedom of choice. If a being is compelled to act according to the mind of another, and has no mind of his own, he is an automaton, and not worth loving. Such personalities God did create, and we are specimens of them; we certainly have freedom of choice; we can obey or disobey God. So that the favorite assertion of "Scientists" is not true, God is not all.

When He will say, and is saying, "Depart from Me ye cursed into everlasting fire prepared for the devil and his angels," He declares that there are beings in existence with whom He has no part, and in whom He does not and cannot reside. God is Spirit, but God is not all. Whether what is not God can be asserted to be Spirit or not, we cannot say. Mrs. Eddy, however, is less cautious. On page 230 she affirms: "God never created matter, for there is nothing in Spirit out of which matter could be made." This entirely depends upon what Spirit is, and what are its qualities and capabilities.

Suppose we allow that Spirit is substance. When Mrs. Eddy says, page 230, that "Spirit is the only substance," she probably expresses a greater truth than she at all imagines; indeed, the next words show she has not an inkling of the possible truth of her assertion that "Spirit is the only substance, the invisible and indivisible God."

To be able to at all think clearly upon this occult subject we must be careful to discriminate between Spirit and Life. When we say Spirit is substance, we mean that it is an existence which lends itself to the offices of Life. Substance is that which "stands under" and gives support to something else. We may even say that Spirit is to a spiritual being what flesh is to a human being. This, indeed, S. Paul distinctly says: "There is a natural body and there is a spiritual body," I. Cor. xv., 44; but the word he used for "natural" would be literally rendered by "soulical," if there was such a word; that is, a body of which the soul is the vitality, the animal body. So the life, when it is a denizen of an immaterial or spiritual world, needs some substance of which to construct a body wherein and whereby it may transact the business of that world — "a spiritual body."

It seems probable that the life assumes for itself three bodies, each of them necessary in the three states which we are to inhabit. As we are now, here in this material world, we have a body of the same sort of matter as the planet on which we live. "The Lord God formed man of the dust of the ground."

Shortly we shall "shuffle off this mortal coil." What "body" will the life then occupy?" The spiritual body, S. Paul tell us; that is, a body of the nature of that spiritual world, where it will await the day of the Resurrection. Then it will again occupy a third body, adapted to the altered conditions which have brought about "the new heavens and the new earth." We have been granted some insight of this mysterious subject in seeing the changes to which the body of the Lord was subject. When He died, He certainly carried with Him his personality. The man who was crucified on his right hand no doubt recognized Him in Paradise; he must have been able to do so, otherwise the Lord's assurance, "This day thou shalt be with Me in Paradise," would have been little else than a phrase without definite meaning. Our Blessed Lord doubtless would appear the same man to him in Paradise as he saw Him on Calvary. Abraham and Joshua and Daniel, and the disciples, and 'the spirits' in prison, and those to whom He showed Himself after his resurrection, and S. Stephen and S. Paul and S. John, after his glorification, all saw the same man. His personal appearance was no doubt always the same, only under various conditions suitable to its environment, it was a 'vile' body or a 'glorified' body; but always the body of the Son of God, through which the Deity, ever unseen, expressed Himself to the beings He was then dwelling with.

The qualities of the resurrection body of the Lord ought to make "Scientists," and the ordinary kind of Scientists, more careful what assertions they use about matter. The material of that body evidently possessed other qualities than those which describe the matter with which we are familiar. It was not a phantom shape. Thomas doubtless could have put his finger into the print of the nails, and have thrust his hand into the gaping spear-wound in his side. It evidently was not seen by reflected light. It was recognized by another sort of light, perhaps that kind of light which illumines the other world, where they need not the sun to lighten them; moreover, it could only be seen when He willed it. No one, saving those who 'knew' Him, appears to have been able to see Him. It was only to his own that He ever 'shewed Himself' after his resurrection, and the power of recognition had something to do with the condition of their own faith, for when He met all his Galilæan disciples we are told all the five hundred saw Him, 'but some doubted.' His body still retained some qualities in common with the material of which this world is made; his voice moved the air and made sound; and He ate before them 'a piece of a broiled fish and an honey comb.'

Mrs. Eddy, no doubt to ward off the very natural suggestion that if matter is nothing but an illusion, it were folly to persist in the delusion that food is necessary to maintain what is nothing, declares, "We need more goodness." Now, I hope she would not suggest that our Blessed Lord was not actual 'Righteousness' itself; and yet He was pleased to eat; so that it is not a question of 'goodness' whether we can do without food.

Our Lord's body could pass through closed doors and walls; it could appear and vanish at will; and at last, in no chariot of fire, but by its own capability, it ascended into heaven. It evidently was either not subservient to the law of gravitation, or completely under the control of the will. This gives us a glimpse of another kind of matter, a kind which is much nearer the condition of the substance of the spiritual world. This, we believe, shall be the condition of our bodies when we shall rise from our graves, for we are assured 'we shall be like Him.'

There are certain hints in this direction which science has of late whispered which are little less than exciting. We have long known that the whole universe is filled with a fluid which physicists have agreed to call ether. It is the oscillations of this ether which cause in us the sensation of light. We can measure the lengths of these oscillations, or waves; we know the exact number which must occur in a second to produce a certain color. It would occupy the whole of the population of the United States, counting for twelve hours a day, nearly six months to count the number of waves of ether which must impinge upon the retina of the eye in one second to give the sensation of violet light for one short moment. Certain mathematical conditions seem to require that, to allow of the prodigious velocity with which waves of light traverse the ether, this ether shall have something like a pressure of 70,000 pounds on each square inch of surface. That is to say, the whole universe is moving, not in empty space, but in a transparent, impalpable, imponderable something, ether, more dense than almost any solid with which we are familiar. It is practically certain that the particles of matter are in violent movement; that that which appears to us silent and motionless is really in indescribable commotion, greatly accelerated by any rise of temperature. Lord Kelvin, the greatest living authority on such subjects, suggested what is known as "The Vortex Theory," that matter itself is composed of vortices, discs or rings, of this ether, in varying conditions of movement and compression, and there are mathematical considerations which again support this theory. Here, then, is a purely physical conception of the universe that is startling. This ether, which cannot be seen or handled, and which is imponderable, under certain conditions becomes matter. Matter is simply a term for ether in these particular conditions. Ether is the only substance. Substitute the word Spirit for the word Ether in the foregoing, and the words of Mrs. Eddy are truly prophetic, "Spirit is the only substance."

Pondering on this wonderful subject, the Boston Sybil, oppressed with her mighty mission, on page 225 of "the little book," wrote:

> The individuality of spirit is unknown, and thus a knowledge of it is left either to human conjecture or to the revelation of "Divine Science."

We still wait for the revelation; and in the meantime we deal with matter, as food, clothing, and even dollar bills, as Mrs. Eddy herself does, and advises her pupils, the Healers, to do likewise!

CHAPTER IX.

FORGIVENESS OF SIN.

THE grand distinguishing feature of the Gospel of Jesus Christ is the doctrine of the forgiveness of sin. No philosophy which ever laid serious claim to the attention of men has ever proposed a way by which the consequences of wrong-doing in the past might be averted, and the present inclination to do wrong again taken away. No religious teacher on earth ever boldly proclaimed to his fellow-men that by following his advice, they might be rid at once of the future consequences and present power of sin, but Jesus Christ. He, and He alone of men, ventured to say, "Come unto Me all ye that are weary and heavy laden and I will give you rest"—rest from 'the burdens of the way' and the fear of future retribution. That this is no vain Gospel is witnessed to by thousands in every generation. Jesus Christ has never been without witnesses to the wonderful result of 'coming unto Him.'

His people 'praise God in the fires;' they 'sing songs in the night;' they are 'filled with the joy and peace of the Holy Ghost;' they are 'in' the world but not 'of' the world; they walk on air. Read the present evidence of missionaries all over the world; read the story of John Paton, who is to-day on the island of Aniwa, in the New Hebrides, and there see how a whole island of brutal cannibals became in eight years transformed into a peaceful, loving, joyous community, by the Gospel of Jesus Christ; or go to the nearest Salvation Army captain and ask him to show you a man or a woman who a few months ago was living in dirt and shame, and you may now see 'a new creature,' with a changed nature and a changed face. The minister of every church ought to be able to point you out here and there one who had suddenly 'touched Christ,' and was walking 'in the light of life,' with a halo of very glory about them, the peace and joy of the Holy Ghost. This is why miracles are no longer necessary.

The 'signs' that the Gospel of Christ is 'the power of God unto salvation' are all round us. To change a whole nature is a much more astonishing work than to open the eyes of a blind man. This is done every day by the simple, straightforward statement of the Gospel, and its whole-hearted acceptance. It is by 'taking God at his word,' and 'believing' what He says, that our 'sins are forgiven by the sacrifice of Jesus Christ;' that we 'yield ourselves unto God;' then the life of Christ—that is, Christ himself—'comes into us and abides with us.' This is the change which comes in conversion, and the astonishing effect of it can be explained in no other way. It then follows, that if the soul becomes vitalized by the life of Christ, so that the words of S. Paul are experimentally realized: 'The life that I now live in the flesh I live by Christ's faith, and when Christ, who is my life, shall appear, then shall I also appear with Him in glory,' Gal. ii., 20; if the assertion of S. John comes true, 'He that is born of God sinneth not, for *his seed* remaineth in him;' then it must be that the actual 'life' of the Lord Jesus Christ is in the believer; and whatever that life did, or will do, the person that has it, also did, and will do! This is the way we are 'planted together into His death,' in the past; and by this absolute union with Christ, we even now 'sit together with Him in heavenly places.' In fine, we are veritable members of his body, bone of his bone, flesh of his flesh; one with Christ, and Christ with us. Astounding as it may seem, nevertheless it is an inevitable consequence of 'the law of this life,' that whatever Christ is or has, that, and nothing less, is ours; "All things are yours, and you are Christ's, and Christ is God's."

This is the Gospel Paul preached; now see what a pitiful travesty of this magnificent revelation is "Christian Science." If Mrs. Eddy and company discarded the Bible, and honestly declared that they shewed unto us 'a more excellent way,' we should at least know by what to estimate their offer. But professing to 'take the Bible for their text-book,' and characterizing themselves as "Christian Scientists," they mislead unwary souls and palm off upon them 'another Gospel,' which has no salvation in it, and they well deserve the anathema S. Paul pronounces against them.

The Christian reader of the books of Mrs. Eddy, and Mrs. Cramer, and Mr. Henry Wood, and the other writers of the cult, soon becomes aware that none of them have any conception of the real nature of sin. It is never more than casually mentioned, and is always spoken of as a flaw of the disposition, and never as the deep-seated leprosy of the nature. On page 345 Mrs. Eddy gives us her opinion on this vital question: "When mortals once admit that evil confers no pleasure, they turn from it;" which is not true. How many a man have I seen 'tied and bound with the chain of his sin,' with bitter tears cursing and loathing the strong drink which he detested and yet loved, and could not turn from, although it not only gave him no pleasure, but was bringing on him and his swift and sure desolation; but to proceed:

> "Divine Science" adjusts the balance as Jesus adjusted it. Science removes the penalty, only by first removing the sin, which incurs the penalty. This is the sense of divine pardon which I understand to mean God's method of destroying sin.

How can 'Science' remove a penalty by removing a sin which already has been committed? If "Divine Science" can turn back the shadow on the sun dial, and cause yesterday to be lived over again, with the experience it yielded, then we can understand how the sin might be 'removed,' by preventing it ever being committed. It is mere childishness, if not something infinitely worse, to propose to remit sin, which the recording angel has registered, by 'removing it.' This is not "God's method of destroying sin."

Sin is the very defection of our nature. This nature descends from parent to child by means of blood, "which is the life thereof," an assertion constantly repeated in the Old Testament. As long as this current of life descends, so long must the beings who live by it be a sinful race, 'dead unto God in trespasses and sins,' without eternal life. But into the line of descent came the Son of God. Mrs. Eddy says, p. 334: "Jesus was the offspring of Mary's self-conscious communion with God," which means nothing. Jesus Christ was "conceived of the Holy Ghost, born of the Virgin Mary." The words of the angel state all that the human mind can understand of the mighty undertaking. "The Holy Ghost shall come upon thee, and the power of the Highest shall overshadow thee, therefore that Holy thing which shall be born of thee (that holy-begotten thing), shall be called the Son of God." So it was that his nature was the Deity, and his body was of the flesh of man.

In his body ran the blood of Adam's race. On Calvary He parted with that blood, but by virtue of his Divine nature He lived through the catastrophe of human death, and came back to life still with a body of this flesh, but without that blood by which only could be the continuance of the sinful nature of fallen man. He carefully referred to this, when allaying the fear of his disciples the night of his resurrection: 'A spirit hath not flesh and bones, as ye see I have.' He did not use the ordinary phrase, 'flesh and blood;' there was no blood in his body. The wounds were open, but bloodless. This is the reason of that well-known assertion, strikingly made by the shedding of the blood of the Sacrificial Victim, and put into words by the inspired writer, "Without the shedding of blood there is no remission of sin."

This is the Gospel S. Paul preached: "Jesus Christ and Him crucified," and this is not the Gospel of "Divine Science." Mrs. Eddy says, p. 227:

> The efficacy of the Crucifixion lies in the practical affection and goodness it demonstrated for mankind. The material blood of Jesus was no more efficacious to cleanse from sin when it was

shed upon the accursed tree, than it was when it was flowing in his veins.

Page 327:

Final deliverance from error . . . . is not reached by pinning one's faith to another's vicarious effort. Whosoever believeth that wrath is righteous cannot understand God.

Page 328:

One sacrifice, however great, is insufficient to pay the debt of sin.

Page 345:

Another's suffering cannot lessen our own liability. Did the martyrdom of Savonarola make the crimes of his implacable enemies less criminal?

No! but Savonarola was not 'the Lamb of God which taketh away the sins of the world.'

Page 229:

The invisible Christ was incorporeal, whereas Jesus was a corporeal or bodily existence. This dual personality of the seen and the unseen, the Jesus and the Christ, continued until the Master's ascension; and then the human, the corporeal concept, or Jesus, disappeared; while the invisible, the spiritual idea, or the Christ, continued.

Let us finally turn to the text-book of the "Christian Scientists," the Bible, and learn what it says:

"The love of Christ constraineth us; because we thus judge, that if one died for all, then were all dead; and that He died for all, that they which live should not henceforth live unto themselves, but unto Him which died for (in the place of) them," I. Cor. v., 14.

"He hath made Him to be sin for us, who knew no sin; that we might be made the righteousness of God in Him," I. Cor. v., 21.

"God, sending his own Son, in the likeness of sinful flesh, and for sin, condemned sin in the flesh," Rom. viii., 3.

"Once, in the end of the world, hath He appeared to put away sin, by the sacrifice of Himself. . . . Christ was once offered to bear the sins of many," Heb. ix., 26–28.

"We are sanctified through the offering of the body of Jesus Christ once for all. . . . By one offering He hath perfected forever them that are being sanctified," Heb. x., 10–14.

"Who in his own self bare our sins in his own body on the tree, that we, being dead to sins, should live unto righteousness; by whose stripes ye were healed," I. Pet. ii., 24.

"Christ hath suffered for us in the flesh," I. Pet. iv., 1.

"The blood of Jesus Christ, his Son, cleanseth us from all sin," I. Joh. i., 7.

"He is the propitiation for our sins; and not for ours only, but also for the sins of the whole world."

"Surely He hath borne our griefs and carried our sorrows; and we did esteem Him stricken, smitten of God, and afflicted. But He was wounded for our transgressions, He was bruised for our iniquities; the chastisement of our peace was upon Him; and with his stripes we are healed. . . . The Lord hath laid on Him the iniquity of us all. It pleased the Lord to bruise Him; He hath put Him to grief; when Thou shalt make his soul an offering for sin, He shall see his seed, He shall prolong his days, and the pleasure of the Lord shall prosper in his hand," Isaiah liii., 4, 6, 10.

It was thus that 'The Son of Man,' the epitome of

humanity, placed himself in our stead, and 'slew the enmity' which separated the human race from God and Holiness, by suffering death; pouring out his blood as a sacrifice for sin. In Him we all died, and 'He that is dead is freed (justified) from sin;' hence, as S. Paul writes, in Romans vi., 'we are dead to sin;' we 'were baptized into his death;' we, 'being planted together, have grown into conformity with his death;' our old man (our Adam nature) was crucified with Him that the body of sin might be rendered powerless; 'we died together with Christ;' all these expressions, taken out of a single chapter, are only to be understood in the light of the fact, that Jesus Christ was the second Adam, and that as surely as we all died in Adam, so we all participate in the deeds of the life of the second Adam, if only we make living union with Him and become 'in Christ.'

Side by side with this marvellous expression of the Gospel of the Grace of God, the salvation of sinners by the incarnation and sacrifice of the Son of God, place the solitary passage to which the index of the text-book of "Christian Science" refers us. Mrs. Eddy knew she must say something of the great undertaking of Jesus Christ, sin-bearing; she knew she was writing for people who 'called themselves Christians,' and they must have some explanation of a doctrine they pretended to hold, but of whose wonderful and transforming grace they had had no personal experience; for no one but a counterfeit Christian could a second time read this paragraph. And I appeal to those who are not wholly reprobate, whose eyes the God of this world hath not wholly blinded, to read this passage on p. 358, and say, in the light of the verses I have above quoted from the Word of God, which alone reveals to us the mystery of the Cross, if this sentence, from the pen of the high-priestess of their profession, is not senseless blasphemy!

Jesus bore our sins in his own body. He knew the mortal error which constitutes the material body, and could destroy that error; but at the time when Jesus felt our infirmities, he had not conquered all the beliefs of the flesh, or his sense of material life, nor had he risen to his final demonstration of spiritual power.

CHAPTER X.

CONCLUSION.

THERE are many other subjects treated of in this book of 'Science and Health,' all of which are as far from the truth as these with which I have dealt, but we have seen sufficient to brand this gospel as 'another gospel,' and not in any sense the Gospel of Jesus Christ. Many persons have tried it, and found it a broken cistern which held no water of life. Several such persons I know, and I asked one of them to write her experience of "Christian Science." She is a lady who is singularly well read; who possesses one of the most capacious memories I have ever found; who for long gave herself to all that 'mind culture' which is so sought after by the women of this generation. God led her out of darkness into his glorious light through the ministry of this Church; so that she is a competent witness to the comparative values of the Gospel of "Christian Science" and the Gospel S. Paul preached.

"My life has been a busy one, in professional work, which required me to spend all my spare time in study. Religions and philosophies chiefly engaged my attention. One by one these failed to be conclusive or restful. 'The Spirit of God moved upon the face of the waters.' So now in the soul of man,

Light must reveal the chaos and create the desire for order ('as it was in the beginning, is now.') In my chaotic state of mind, 'Christian Science' appealed to me as being more spiritual than most religions. It offered much enjoyment to a person of trained mind, quick perceptions, and some degree of culture. But from these lessons I went out among the people who were burdened with daily toil, sins and sickness. They could not read the books I lent them. They could not understand the lessons. Yet their hearts were hungry, like mine, for food. And when I asked my teacher how the scrub-woman or the twelve-hours-a-day fireman could find this perpetual elevation of soul necessary to the faith, the answer was: 'They can't, till they rise out of that life." Then there were the sick and the sin-sick. What could my 'Christian Science' say to this girl, hopelessly pleading for peace? 'Sin has no existence—sickness no reality;' could I say that? Not in the very face of her misery! I dared not say that."

"And I began to wonder, Has 'Christian Science' anything like that wondrous word, 'Neither do I condemn thee; go in peace?' Everywhere this problem met me. And the answer of the teacher was: 'You can do such people no good. They are not yet ready for the Truth.' Because of this growing un-christian lack of sympathy in me, I began to doubt the value of the 'Christian Science' Faith."

"It was said of Jesus, 'the common people heard Him gladly.' This new faith might still be the truth of *Science*, but I began to omit the first word of the name."

"The greater reason for my rejection of this religion, was the internal evidence of the spirit, in the torture of conscience. 'Christian Science' claimed to be based upon the Bible as its authority. I read the first great commandment, 'Thou shalt love the Lord thy God with all thy heart,' etc. But the teachers objected to 'Lord' as implying personality. I must love with all my heart—Principle. I could think of the dear ones long dead, as at rest in Nature, sooner than at rest in Principle. This Principle, was pure Holiness and Truth. Then came the question: Do I honestly love, with all my heart—Holiness? And Conscience, not wholly dead, of course answered, No! What then? 'Science' answered: 'You must deny utterly all sin in yourself. You cannot sin. There is no such thing as sin. It is unreal.' But the torture of conscience was very real."

"Then I read again in my Bible, 'This is life Eternal to know Thee, the only true God, and Jesus Christ.' I stopped there."

"'Christian Science' had told me of God, that is, Principle. It had told me of Christ; that, too, is Principle. But of Jesus, 'Science' had said: 'He was a living person, who once walked and talked and loved as we do.' Here was what the hungry heart wanted; a living Friend to know and believe in. The 'Scientist' said, 'Jesus, the man.' But the Bible does not separate the words; it says 'Jesus Christ, whom to know is Life Eternal.' And my heart quickly answered to this, 'If I may only know Him!' And I began to read the Gospel story of Jesus Christ, and there was then something to say to tired, sick people. They could understand those stories of that life in Galilee."

"'Science' proved itself a beautiful thing for sunny days; but it failed me in my sorest need. And so when people tell me they are happy in the study of 'Christian Science,' my heart replies, 'Yes! you are happy, while as yet you see no end.' But it has an end. And He has said: 'This (not some other faith) is Life Eternal, to know Him and Jesus Christ.'"

"The difference is as light to darkness; He led me out of darkness into his marvellous light, and now I know the reality of what S. Paul tells us, that our hearts cannot conceive the joy God has in store for those who love Him. And my daily prayer is, that all who are seeking peace, through 'Christian Science' teachings, may be led on through that desert to the Waters of Life."

The truth that there is in "Christian Science" is this: The healings it affects are the natural consequences of the power of mind over matter, thought and will over body. The processes it adopts happen to be peculiarly favorable to direct 'suggestion' to the affected part. The sitting quiet; the banishing from the mind all extraneous subjects; shutting the eyes; the soft voice of the healer; the repetition of meaningless sentences, the intelligence is not stirred by them, there is nothing which can cause the mind to work; it is a sort of stroking the mind until it drowsily purrs, leaving the repeated 'suggestion' potent; this is a mode of mesmerizing. All this contributes to stimulate that nerval force, or at least to allow it free course, which, in certain classes of disease, is all that is needful for a return to health.

We hear of the peace "Christian Scientists' affirm they acquire. This is the result of that meditative quiet which is the great resource of the profession. The Quakers attained it. They spoke softly, they walked slowly, they sat in silence long, their dress was of soft fabrics and of neutral colors, and all this contributed to allay that irritation which the attrition of every-day life is so apt to produce.

Let any one deliberately retire for only half an hour, daily, and sit still, communing with their own hearts, and doing nothing, looking at nothing; and it is astonishing how quickly will come evenness of disposition.

And in fine, though I say it with a sad heart, one main reason of the spread of this delusion is, that it gives a host of people a means of notoriety and even emolument, who without it, would neither attain the one nor gain the other. It very rarely appeals either to the really educated on one hand, or to the uneducated on the other; but its natural habitat is in that vast class of people who lie between, who have little cultivated the power of thought, and cannot keep in mental view two ideas at a time, and therefore are unable to draw sound deductions.

It is a very curious sight, and one which affords much serious reflection to the sociologist, to see such a number of intelligent people, listening constantly to assertions their hourly experience contradicts; being assured of the power of the theory to banish sickness, when the vast majority of attempted cures wholly fail; to hear them ever lauding self-repression, but never doing those works of kindness and charity which are the usual offspring of unselfishness; and to see them gathering to listen to 'Readings,' which are nonsensical. To the sincere Christian, it is a sad and painful sight to see people 'hewing out for themselves broken cisterns, which can contain no water,' when at their very doors there is bursting and bubbling that well of 'the water of life,' which the God, who loves us with an everlasting love, has graciously opened in our midst for 'sin and for uncleanness;' wherefore, then, dost thou not ask of Him and He will give thee living water, that thou mayest drink and live forever?

This almost cursory examination of a deeply interesting subject has brought under our notice much food for reflection. Here is a theory which has been accepted by 200,000 persons, and is by them being propagated with an ardour which is not a little astonishing. A large proportion of these thousands have undoubtedly been relieved from ailments more or less irritating. In very many of these cases, ample opportunity was given to the ordinary medical practice to try its nostrums, and without effect.

We believe an honest perusal of the foregoing pages, especially if the investigation be continued in the direction indicated, will lead to the conviction that all these cures have been of disorders due to some disorganization of the nerval system. That this masterly power of nerve force, which holds so high a position in the commonwealth of our bodies, is eminently under the governance of the will. That this will is not always under the direction of consciousness, but appears to be also the executive of that department of the mind which may be called 'the subjective mind.' That this mind can receive suggestions, and put them into effect even better than when consciousness, and reason, its trained servitor, direct the will to require the obedience. That if when in an hypnotic sleep, this 'subjective mind' receives a suggestion, of which nothing is remembered upon awakening, it will put it into practice, if it possibly can, without the intervention of the conscious will.

And more than this, this power can be invoked, when the subject is not actually put to sleep mesmerically; but that when the mind is partially unconscious, then the 'subjective mind,' liberated, as it were, from the necessity of being in attendance upon the active intelligence, follows the direction of the 'suggestion' impressed upon it, and goes about to set to rights the nerval defection.

It would be strange, indeed, if a profession ever upon the alert to discover remedies for disorders, and alleviations for distress, should refuse to learn from the lessons that "Christian Science" undoubtedly teaches. It is high time that, in the medical curriculum, room should be made for the study of the power of the will to rectify bodily disorder. It has been said that hypnotism is too dread a power, and as yet too uncontrollable, to be used indiscriminately; but how many poisons are in daily use by the medical practitioner, and in his educated hand are of the greatest therapeutic benefit? Let the men whose life-work it is to gather for us every healing experience, give their attention, to dissect out of the woof and web of this blurred fabric of "Christian Science" the golden thread which leads to the secret of the cures so numerously performed, and let another department be definitely added to therapeutics. Meanwhile, let the law require that no "Christian Science" healer, or others of that sort, shall undertake to treat any sick person who has not consulted a properly authorized practitioner, to ascertain the nature of the disease, that it be not of a sort likely to terminate fatally.

For let death occur, and whatever the remorse, the traveller will not return from that bourne.

This authoritative investigation would tend to refer the curative power to its proper source, and deliver many well-meaning people from accepting teachings at variance with those truths upon which they have always been taught to place dependence. It would, indeed, seem that S. Paul had in his mind erratic theories of this sort when he wrote to Timothy: "Now the Spirit speaketh expressly that in the latter times some shall depart from the faith, giving heed to seducing spirits, and doctrines of devils."

There are those who say, that it is of little moment what we believe, if only we are in earnest and live decently. But to reach any destination chiefly depends upon the accuracy of our knowledge as to whether the road we are travelling will lead us to the place whither we would go. Energy, determination and perseverance on the wrong road, can only lead us further away from the goal. How wrong the religious ventures of Mrs. Eddy are, we have seen. They are all the more dangerous because they adopt the air and language of Scripture. They profess to take their whole authority from the Word of God, and seem to readily agree with the dicta of revelation. But, as the wisest of the sons of men well said: "There is a way that seemeth right unto a man: but the end thereof are the ways of death," Proverbs xvi., 25.

www.ingramcontent.com/pod-product-compliance
Lightning Source LLC
Chambersburg PA
CBHW031348160426
43196CB00007B/768